MY FRUIT IS MAGICAL:

OVERCOME 8 LIES THAT KEEP YOU SINGLE OR UNHAPPY
YOU CAN HAVE THE LOVE STORY YOU WANT!

LILY B. DONKOR

Copyright © 2020 by Lilian Donkor

All rights reserved. This book or any portion thereof may not be reproduced or used in any manner whatsoever without the express written permission of the publisher except for the use of brief quotations in a book review.

Portions of this book are personal stories. Certain names and identifying characteristics have been changed.

Printed in the United States of America

First Printing, 2020

ISBN: 978-1-7348566-0-6 (hardback)
ISBN: 978-1-7348566-1-3 (paperback)
ISBN: 978-1-7348566-2-0 (ebook)

Book cover by Nfinite Design

The Barning Company Publishing
lovenyou.org

To the first man who owned my heart, Uyi Ediagbonya
To the last man who ever will, David Donkor

table
OF CONTENTS

AN INTRODUCTION 1

CHAPTER 1
I NEED TO HAVE FUN NOW 15

CHAPTER 2
HE HAS TO LIKE ME FOR WHAT'S ON THE
INSIDE FIRST. 31

CHAPTER 3
HE MUST BE ABLE TO PROVIDE FOR ME 41

CHAPTER 4
I NEED TO BE ESTABLISHED FIRST. 53

CHAPTER 5
MY FRUIT IS MAGICAL 65

CHAPTER 6
WE DON'T NEED TO LABEL IT TO MAKE IT
REAL 79

CHAPTER 7
TWO CAN PLAY THAT GAME 91

CHAPTER 8
A RELATIONSHIP IS SUPPOSED TO MAKE ME HAPPY 101

CONCLUSION
YOUR LOVE STORY 113

ACKNOWLEDGMENTS 117
BIBLIOGRAPHY 119
ABOUT THE AUTHOR 123

EVERY JOURNEY BEGINS WITH COMMITMENT

An Introduction

Every journey begins with commitment. It takes a commitment to start a diet regimen, a business, or a relationship, and an even greater commitment to follow through until the desired results are achieved. I have made a commitment to myself and am now making this commitment to you: to share real-life love stories and the truths about what it takes to find, develop, and sustain love, particularly within the framework of marriage.

Before I got married, I felt I had a fairly reasonable expectation of what married life would be like. I believed marriage is a union between a man and woman who love each other. I believed making a marriage enjoyable and functional required both parties to commit to a lifestyle of continuous communication and compromise. I figured if you earnestly love your spouse and show them the same care you show toward yourself, you should be absolutely fine. Although not completely off track, I had no personal marriage experience—nor did I know enough married couples' stories to use as a frame of reference. As much as I was curious and enjoyed learning about other people's experiences—from diets they found effective, to how they found the courage to follow their dreams—I did not feel comfortable asking random strangers to tell me their love stories because I wanted to learn from their experiences. I now feel this lack of access to valuable information is a general problem. Why is there not a resource available for anyone interested in learning from, or interacting with, other married couples? An available resource that does not require you to sign up as a member of an exclusive club or attend a pricey three-day marriage workshop.

I wrote this book to fill this information gap, and more specifically to debunk eight dating and matrimony myths on: sexuality, finances, beauty and tradition, among others. Each chapter of this book will focus on one of eight myths (I have no doubt there are many more). I will provide you with practical advice and a narrative of an actual relationship that hinged on that myth. Further, I'll invite you to watch a video at lovenyou.org or Instagram (@lovenyoubrand), of a married couple whose story debunks that myth, or of men providing the male perspective on the myth. I also wrote this book to introduce you to Love'n You, a resource designed to help you identify obstacles and/or behaviors in your self-love and relationship journey that may be keeping you from reaching a goal, maintaining love or self-actualization. You can learn more about For Better and other products at lovenyou.org and @lovenyoubrand on social media. Love'n You provides you with access to the stories and journeys of various married couples, giving you the freedom to learn about different kinds of marriages in a time, space, and pace of your own choosing. You get the valuable benefit of cross-referencing your beliefs about marriage with the realities of actual married couples.

MY FRUIT IS MAGICAL

I authored this book for women who desire to tie the knot one day and would like to get a sense of what to expect in marriage. I wrote it for the young women I mentor who deliberate on, and conduct research, before making major decisions. I wrote it for the twenty-first century woman who wants to benefit from other people's perspectives but does not have the luxury of the required time to meet and quiz dozens of couples. I am happy to have had the privilege of writing this book and am convinced you will find it of immeasurable value.

I challenge you to enter into a short-term commitment with me as you read this book. Commit to approaching each chapter, relationship narrative, and accompanying video with the intent to be fully engaged. By doing so, you will allow yourself to experience the full spectrum of what that chapter has to offer and maybe even challenge some of your unchecked assumptions. I have selected specific real-life stories for each chapter you can connect with. I understand there is a wide range of varying experiences for each topic, but for the sake of time and practicality, I used only one story per chapter. Additional stories are available online @lovenyoubrand.

Each chapter explores the prevailing myths keeping us single longer than we desire, or unhappy in current relationships. A few myths undermining some women's ability to enjoy lasting romantic relationships, include the following: "I have to have fun now; I need to be established first; and a relationship is supposed to make me happy." Some of the eight myths also apply to those who are in a relationship or married, but still engage in beliefs that keep them discontented and unfulfilled.

This book is a male-informed, female-contributed, self-experienced journey I am pleased to share with you. Every single story and insight has been shaped by one or more of these three factors.

LILY B. DONKOR

The Male Perspective

Since an early age, I have had the opportunity to observe the male outlook on relationships. From nine to nineteen, I was raised in a single-parent home by my father until he passed away. I have four sisters and two brothers, of which I am the eldest daughter. Being the first girl, my dad and I had a very special relationship. I am a self-proclaimed "queen of all daddy's little girls." In my early teens, I not only knew, but also downright understood, there were truthfully different consequences for identical acts committed by the sexes. When I say I understood, I mean I was past questioning why there was a difference in how boys and girls were treated. For me, it was not a matter of fairness or equality. I understood what I needed to do as a female in order to achieve my desired goals. I understood I had to employ different means to arrive at the same outcomes as my brother. I was not hung up on comparing my responsibilities versus rewards with his. I was focused on how I could have fun, get good grades, and get away with some mischief but still remain daddy's little girl.

The truth was, I had benefited from perks my brother never had, and I enjoyed being a girl—imposed gender norms and all. My goal was to embrace being me, a girl, and use every advantage that came with it. This was my advantage. (Let us be clear: my father was not afraid to lay down the law, as you will find out in later chapters).

My dad and I would talk about almost anything, and I seemed to have a maturity about me that facilitated easy discussions even at that time. Since my father was not married for some of the ten years he raised my siblings and me, he dated. Yes, he dated a lot. I observed his interactions with the women he dated, their behaviors toward him, and eventually the perceptible differences between the women who did not last and the one he eventually married. Occasionally, he would jokingly predict how long a relationship would last and why it would not work. I mostly just observed, not necessarily with his permission or knowledge.

I occasionally played the role of wingman for my brother, who is two years older than me. He would include me in a few of his girl-getting schemes. I began to recognize the language he used when he respected a woman versus how he behaved when she left little to be desired. And because we had a close relationship, he would "educate" me on male dating behavior and secrets, some of which my female emotions caused me to dismiss from my mind when I needed them most. But I can still rehearse most of his lessons in my mind to date. By virtue of our close relationship, I was usually around and got along with most of his friends. They would seldom modify their behavior for my sake or benefit, and I appreciated that. I had access to unfiltered information about relationships from a male perspective.

In high school, university, and postgrad, my closest friends were male, although I have a few cherished female relationships I still hold dear to this day. My male friends endowed me with great awareness of the male outlook. I respect and cherish the male view on love so much that three of the four people who read and loved the manuscript of this book were men. We need to know what and how men think if we are interested in making them part of our love story.

Before the idea came about to begin writing this book, I had been fortunate enough to speak briefly at a workshop for a women's conference. I have attended this conference for many years, four of which I attended as a delegate and first lady of a local church. I had been married for six years to a minister (now ten years) and had counseled singles, couples, and divorced people alongside my husband. The topic I addressed was "Where Are All the Good Men?" Women were coming to hear me speak and advise them about eligible men: where to find them and how to eventually secure love with them. Because I knew the demographics of the attendees, I was certain I would have both the pleasure and pressure of speaking to women twice my age, some of whom had been in multiple marriages. I took my responsibility very seriously! The only logical thing for me to do was to go to the core source: I had long and hard conversations with my male colleagues, friends, and distant relatives. I asked and polled married men, single men, divorced men, blue and white-collar professionals, the unemployed, Caucasian, Indian, and African men—you name it. It was important I did the topic justice for the sake of every woman who had chosen to come and listen to me speak. They needed to know where the eligible men were, and I needed the men to draw me the map.

The Female Contribution

I am not sure where my interest in relationships and human behavior stemmed from, but in the last few years, it has become my passion. For me, deriving pleasure from learning about this subject is one thing; but the excitement really begins when I help others navigate the terrain of relationships. Because of the male perspectives I have mentioned earlier, I am able to examine relationships and draw meaningful insights that other women can act on. In my years as a minister's wife, I have had the privilege of interacting, counseling, and coaching couples at various times of their relationship life cycles. These interactions always serve as teachable moments for me. As much as others come to me expecting some value and insight, my own keenness compels me to elevate my skill set. At any given period of my adult life and for the foreseeable future, I mentor women and am always on the lookout for mentors to challenge my growth. My experiences with these women have guided this book. I have included some candid discussions, as recollected with the aid of journal entries, in the hopes that you would be able to connect with these human experiences.

My Experience with Dating

Lastly, this book is influenced by my own personal journey. This firsthand learning continues to fuel my passion to explore and share real-life love stories. A few notable personal relationships have really made an impression on how I view and approach love. As early as middle school, I would watch as the popular girls talked about their boyfriends. And I would witness during recess what I felt then were displays of "true love." I was fixated on and fascinated by love. Between the ages of twelve to fifteen, I dated and broke up with at least half a dozen boys in my mind. I had my first actual boyfriend when I was fifteen. It lasted all of three weeks, but it was an eventful three weeks. He asked me to be his girlfriend at work one evening, and before I got to school the next morning my best friend told me he was already cheating on me (keep in mind this was before Facebook, Twitter, and Instagram). He apparently already had a girlfriend. After questioning him about it, he cried, denied it, and bought me a pair of Timberland boots, Parasuco jeans, and a shirt. The gifts appeased me for two weeks, but when his "love" did not measure up to the relationships envisioned in my mind, it was time to walk away. The reality of dating, even at that tender age, was disappointing compared to what I expected.

It would be over a year before I dated again, and this relationship lasted for three years. As you can probably imagine, it was transformative for me. It taught me lessons I'm not sure I was ready to learn, but I now happily embrace and use them as a point of reference when interacting with youth at a similar age and stage. My ex-boyfriend and I had broken up and not spoken for months when my father passed away, but we got back together for a week or two right after the funeral. I am certain the deep hurt of just having lost the man I loved most in life caused me to reach for my ex, who I thought was the closest substitute for my huge loss.

In the months and years following my father's death, and soon after the final breakup with my longtime boyfriend, I swore off dating. This time enabled me to study and explore myself candidly and with no holds barred. I lived alone, for the most part, supported myself while in school, and forced myself to journal. I would write down my goals, fears, and insecurities, and would detail the interactions I had with the opposite sex. I would mention the ones I had a casual conversation with, the ones who tried to pick me up (one of whom I dated for a day in a momentary lapse of judgment), and the ones I wanted to get to know better. I would periodically go back and read my journal entries, and in doing so became empowered and confident. Although I longed for love and a relationship, I was bolstered by knowing I had the power to choose what I wanted and when I wanted it!

After almost three years of being happily single, I struck up a friendship with a young man who attended the same university as I did. We knew we were interested in one another and were open to getting to know each other better. He was an international student from a family of affluence. As the days and weeks passed, I began to pick up on his "spoiled rich kid" behavior, but when he made a jest of my decision to be celibate until marriage, I made it clear we could only remain friends. Two years earlier, on my twentieth birthday, I had taken a vow of celibacy not to be broken until I was married (I had actually also vowed not to lose my virginity until

I turned eighteen, a promise I kept even though I started dating my boyfriend of three years when I was sixteen). These experiences and others have helped me prove to myself that we women wield the power, control, and freedom in charting the course we desire in relationships. Because I was so in tune with myself, I was fairly certain of who or what brought out the best in me; I knew most of my weaknesses and had a working knowledge of my capacity to grow. Because of my own fractured family dynamic, I wanted someone from a fairly 'normal' upbringing. I recognized, even then, that I lacked some essential benefits of growing up with both parents in the home. Now that I am blessed with a young family of my own, it is glaringly evident that God's design for the family is best: a father and mother raising children together in the home. The person had to be patient and methodical in their approach to solving issues because I was far from that (my husband, David's influence has definitely moved the needle on my patience meter). I was not eager to get married but was keenly aware of traits I wanted and needed in a life partner. I married an amazing man just two months before my twenty-fifth birthday.

My Experience with God

I would not be painting a complete picture of this time frame in my life if I did not mention where and how I found mental strength and emotional fortitude. For you to fully understand why and how I make most of the decisions I do now, it is important you know what happened in my early twenties. I was born and raised in Nigeria until the age of nine and lived with both of my parents for many of those years. When my parents separated, my father moved to Canada and shortly thereafter, my elder brother and I immigrated to join him permanently. As far

LILY B. DONKOR

back as I can remember, my mother went to church, meaning that we went to church A LOT. When we were not physically at church, mom was praying, singing church songs, or attending other church related functions. I was, therefore, a forced Pentecostal Christian by default (until the age of nine). My father, on the other hand, was an Apathist, a person who is not interested in accepting or rejecting any claims to religion or gods. But because he lived a militant way of life, he liked the routine the catholic mass offered us. Consequently, like clockwork, we would get dressed every Sunday morning for mass. He would give my siblings and me—my brother and three sisters from his second marriage—our offerings, drop us off at the parish for mass then return to pick us up forty-five minutes later. For me, Church attendance up to the age of sixteen was solely out of duty towards my parents. When I turned sixteen and had the option, I chose to sleep in on Sundays. I only went to mass on Christmas and Easter at that stage of my life, just in case there was a God. Attending church on the days of His supposed birth and death seemed respectful enough to me. I had no relationship with, or knowledge of God and I had no desire either way. I had many occasions and invitations from friends and extended family members to attend church. But again, I had no interest. I believed subscribing to a religion meant adhering to its codes of conducts; the do's and don'ts of that faith. And I was not ready to do that. Up to this point in my life, I was directly governed by social laws, parental mandates, and my own conscience, although my own conscience often overruled the first two when there was no oversight. A person's freedom of choice is enormously powerful, and at the same time dangerous. At seventeen, I could make life altering decisions and no one could stop me, but me. That is scary. Just consider for a moment that social laws at the very least are five thousand years old. They have adapted and evolved based on social norms and best practices to what we have now. The parental mandates that governed me were informed by at least a hundred years of family tradition, experience and best practices gathered by my father in his forties. Yet, at seventeen, my conscience and experiences trumped all that. In my mind, I knew better than society and I knew better than my dad. It sounds arrogant and foolish, but that was my reality and my truth up until that point. At twenty, much of that began to change. I was invited and attended a social event at a church in Toronto, and for months after that, I would occasionally stop by out of curiosity. Late 2004, I attended a spiritual retreat hosted by this church and for the first time, I saw myself. Stay with me here. I do not mean this in an airy pretentious way. I mean it in the rawest, jarring, and uncomfortable sense. I relived every traumatic, ugly, and awful experience I had buried in the recesses of my mind; the self-reflective questions forced me to admit my own weakness and the role I played in even the worst moments of my past. And I saw and felt how vulnerable I really was as a person. I came to terms with the limited power I had in the grand scheme of creation, and yet at the same time recognized the strength and power I possessed. I discovered the power I had to choose and change my narrative and my future. I was empowered and emboldened by that weekend retreat program but was forever changed by the new relationship I found and formed with Jesus. This relationship has changed me, and continues to inform who I am, and how I interact with the world around me. It is the knowledge of precisely how God sees me and the fact that Jesus died for me that authenticates the high value of Lily. I do not mean that in an arrogant way. It simply means the way you interact with a Lamborghini Veneno is not the same you would with a Suzuki Sidekick. They are both fine cars in their own rights. However, if they are both clean and in working form, my three-year-old daughter will choose the shinier one. My seven-year-old son who loves and studies cars (like his father) can tell you about every minute detail that contributed to the Veneno's high value. He knows this is not the car to take off-roading unless you do not care what happens to it as a result. My relationship with Christ compels me to constantly ask myself key questions when relating to others around me. It compels me to value others highly and to see them primarily as He sees them before considering what role they serve in my life. I, like you, will always have preferences and personal desires. But knowing that Christ knows me completely and cares for me more deeply than I can, makes it easier to lean more towards His prescription for my love life. Jesus Christ knows me down to the very core of my being and I, therefore, choose to consider His words and way of life higher than my own.

My personal journey has taught me it is important to reconcile fantasies with honest realities. It has taught me that boys lie and boys do also cry. I have learned we have ultimate control over our minds, bodies, and will, and we can give love away freely or award it based on the criteria of our own choosing. My ultimate criteria became the acknowledgement of my worth and my core beliefs. My experiences in navigating my love story and my ongoing curiosity and work in the relationship sphere all set the seal on this book.

I absolutely love studying human relationships, especially with regard to couples. I am energized by learning from different couples and finding out what works for them, what does not, and the experiences that have shaped their relationships. I enjoy reading, watching, or listening to experts on the topic and seeing how their information lines up with the principles I hold dear. But most of all, it is riveting to help an individual figure out how to get from point A to point B in their relationship life.

My aim for you is to change for the better after having taken the time to come on this journey with me. After you have read this book and watched and commented on the accompanying love story videos, I hope you feel more empowered to live out your own love story!

CHAPTER 1
I Need to Have Fun Now

I was set to travel to Toronto for a week to attend and speak at a women's conference in the fall of 2014—the same one I mentioned earlier. Before I booked my flights, one of my university friends who lives in Toronto sent me a message that she would like to go out to grab a bite and catch up. I happened to have other meetings lined up and would need to stay a few days after the conference anyway. I hence told her I would be thrilled to spend some time shooting the breeze.

We gushed over how neither of us had changed at all since university and how fabulous the other person looked. I told her about the conference, and she regretted not being able to attend because of her demanding work schedule. She asked me to share some of my favorite moments from the conference with her. I told her about the gifted keynote speaker of the conference and the wealth of information we received, and I mentioned how nervous I was during my presentation.

LILY B. DONKOR

She joked about how ladies are always curious about relationships to the point of obsession. She was completely in favor of marriage, and in fact planned to get married and start a family someday, but was put off by what she perceived as a preoccupation with marriage. During our brunch date she said, "If they (women) are not in a dating relationship, they wish they were in one. And if they are in one, they wish the relationship was better. And if it is good, they start getting pressured to get married. It is just too much." We agreed about the undue external pressures to settle down. But the conversation got more interesting when she dismissed getting married anytime soon by saying, "I need to live for the moment and have fun now while I'm still young."

I definitely agreed with her that the trend to be with someone and settle down can be all-consuming if you allow it. Most women will agree when you reach a certain age you begin getting an inordinate number of questions about your relationship status, and on occasion, the big question: "When are you getting married?" So, even if marriage is the farthest thought from your mind, someone is bound to nudge it into your consciousness. As a female of Nigerian heritage, I know too well the pressure to get married before the age of thirty—as if thirty is like the best-before date on a gallon of milk: you can consume it after that date, but it is not advisable you do so. The irony is, Nigerian girls are typically not "allowed" to date until we graduate from university. But the moment we do, we had better walk out of that auditorium with our degree and an engagement ring or, at the very least, a committed boyfriend from a good home. So yes, pressure can be too much. But it does not need to be. Here is what I suggest in one word: *Live!*

LIVE!

You may feel the internal and external pressures beginning to mount in your mid-to-late twenties, a period in your life when you begin to earn a decent income for the first time. You no longer have the demands of school on your calendar, and you are not necessarily responsible for anyone else's life. You are as free as you will ever be, and there is a whole world waiting to be explored. So live! Expand your horizons and increase your odds of actually meeting a guy beyond your usual circles. For the present, forget about the social pressure that says you need a ring around that finger when you graduate.

Remember that outlandish business idea? Why not go for it? That social club you liked but resisted joining since you knew no one else there? Join it! Oh, you have never been thirty miles outside of your city? Get a passport! There is a wide world out there waiting to be discovered. And guess what more? That world has *men*: men who did not attend your high school, men who do not know your name, and men who have not dated any of your friends—or enemies. And while you are out there in that great big world trying new cuisine, starting a business venture, or taking a kickboxing class, you just might bump into Mr. Right accidentally, on purpose.

While encouraging you to expand your horizons, the second part of my friend's statement, "I need to live for the moment and have fun now while I'm still young," is troubling. It is troubling because it implies marriage equals the end of fun. I actually think because you are young and have time, you need to be intentional about your relationships. I think of the late teens through the early twenties as the pre-production phase of life. It is the time when you have the most liberty to decide what you really want out of life. You could sit down and design the life you want at this stage. Draw the blueprint. Decide if you want to go to college, where you want to go, and why. Decide what kind of adult you want to be, how you can become the best version of yourself, and how to get there. You can choose where in the state, country, or world you want to live. You can decide if you want to get married and what kind of person fits into your future plan. And because your life is still in pre-production, you can decide what to leave on the cutting room floor.

Because you are young, it is time to be intentional. Being young does not have to mean making a series of strange decisions you spend your late twenties and thirties cleaning up after. Being young should mean "I have the gift of time to plan a future that will knock my socks off." Being young gives you the advantage of having room enough to tweak your plans, perhaps more aggressively than you can in your thirties and forties, when you may have a spouse or children or both, or perhaps an aging or ill family member, along for the ride. The beauty of setting your intended goal when you are young is that you have a certain latitude.

Your goal indicates what you want and how to achieve it, but equally as important, it shows you what you *do not* want.

Whether it is an endless string of parties or completing three years of a degree you loathed in college, wasting time is wasting time. We should be very intentional about our futures. This includes who we want to spend the rest of our lives with, and this starts at the pre-production phase, or exactly where you are now. If you are like most people who want to get married or are married, you intend to have a *happily ever after* marriage, which means you will be married longer than you'll be single. *Hello?* If you live an average human lifespan and desire to be married until death-do-you-part, you will be married longer than your entire single life, in most cases. I want you to consider this while keeping my friend's statement in mind. According to her thinking, all her youthful time, energy, and resources will be focused on making the next few years as pleasurable as possible instead of making the longer stretch of her life what she wants it to be.

My question to you is, where will you invest? I mean in a general sense and in your relationships. Do you really need to spend that $250 on another "on-trend" piece of clothing, or can you invest that money into your future? Will you invest in yet another relationship that forces you to convince yourself that he is interested in more than just sex, or can you hold out for someone who cannot wait to build a life with you? Do you have to go to that party with the same faces, or will you finally start your business? Which phase of your life will get the best of you? Be intentional. Since you are reading this book, I assume marriage or at least a committed relationship is important to you. If it is, I want to assure you that it is never too late. That is the beautiful thing about life: it gives us as many chances as we are willing to accept. You do not have to settle. Plot out how you want the rest of your love story to pan out. What kind of man do you want as your husband? What traits would you like your children's father to have? Who do you want to vacation with, partner with, and share your forever with?

I heard it said, "Marriage is not a word. It is a sentence—a life sentence!!!" Only you can decide whether your life sentence will be spent in a prison or a thousand-acre palace—I mean that both literally and figuratively. Consider the following story.

A Coupling Narrative

Brenda grew up in a very strict religious home. Her parents are of Hindu background (although not currently practicing) and had an arranged marriage in their early twenties. Sonya and Padre, her parents, are a deliriously happy couple and attentive parents. Sonya is a law professor, and Padre is a realtor.

Although she knew her parents had no regrets about their arranged marriage, Brenda wanted to explore and live life in her twenties to the fullest.

As soon as she got accepted into college, she hopped from one party and relationship to another. During this four-year stretch, she and her mother would butt heads about what Sonya referred to as "misplaced enlightenment." Brenda insisted she was on a quest of self-discovery, and allowing herself to experience as much of her world as possible, in ways she deemed fit, was the proper way to do so. The two got along quite well except when the topic of relationships came up. Brenda especially got a kick from getting her mom riled up. If Sonya was eating and left anything on the plate, Brenda would tease her, saying, "Mom, you have such a poor appetite. Don't worry—I'll sample from your plate as well!"

Padre knew to steer clear of them altogether when they began their bouts. Brenda had inherited his temperament, which meant when her mind was made up there was little that could be done to change it. Besides, he did not entirely agree with his wife's approach, but he would keep his opinion to himself.

Brenda did not exactly plan to have sex with as many men as possible. Instead, she wanted to let time and life lead her. She allowed encounters with men to develop unencumbered. If there was chemistry and it happened to lead to sex, then so be it. If it led to coffee and nothing more, that too was perfectly okay with her. She was interested in discovering who she was as a woman, what pleased her, how she pleased men, and what the experience as a whole taught her about herself. She learned that she loved spontaneity, was not too keen on the kinky stuff, and size mattered only to the extent that she knew he was still in there.

She met many wonderful people along the way and built some great social relationships. She met her current best friend and financial mentor during those formative four years.

As much as Brenda teased her mom and grandparents about their culture and customs, she seems to now gravitate toward men from that same "old country" background and upbringing. As she gets older, she is beginning to appreciate extended family gatherings and traditional celebrations. And the more she attends these functions, the greater her interest in men who appreciate traditional values. The kicker now is that many of the men she is attracted to are either already coupled or do not care for the exploring she engaged in in her early twenties. Brenda does not feel the need to lie about her past when the subject of sex comes up in conversations, but she also appreciates that the few guys she has the chance to get to know are more interested in a partner who is not as sexually experienced as she is. She does not regret the life she led. In fact, she would not trade any of the professional relationships and experiences. If she had not spent a weekend at a friend's cabin, she would not have met and struck up a conversation with her current financial mentor. Her spontaneous road trip to Windsor, a four hour drive from Toronto, taught her she was not interested in emotionally attuned men as she thought she was. Her then boyfriend spent most of the time sobbing about his relationship insecurities. Her explorative years yielded some benefits that have helped to shape her mindset about money. On one of the evenings she spent in Windsor, she struck up a conversation with an accountant who was seated at the table next to them in a restaurant. That accountant had now become Brenda's financial mentor and a cherished relationship had developed. As with almost every experience, there can be valuable lessons learnt but that does not mean we must subject ourselves to every experience to learn the lesson. That same knowledge can be gained minus the emotional, psychological, and physical toll. Contrary to the popular adage, experience is NOT the best teacher. A dedication to learn is a better teacher. We all know someone who has refused to learn valuable lessons from repeated detrimental behavior or experiences. Although she does not regret her casual relationships entirely, in hindsight she is not so sure they were valuable or necessary.

By no means am I advocating living a bland and boring life before you get married. What I am saying is this: trying to cram all your fun into a few years and making regrettable choices because you are afraid marriage will rob you of adventure is irrational. Brenda's primary reason for deciding to "have fun while I'm young" was that she was convinced her mother had missed out on opportunities to live and enjoy life as a single female.

> A married couple went out to a nice restaurant to celebrate their fiftieth wedding anniversary. While driving home the wife saw a tear coming from her husband's eye. "Are you

happy that we have spent fifty splendid years together?" she said. He said, "No. I was just thinking about our wedding, and how your father threatened me with a shotgun that if I didn't marry you right then he would have me thrown in prison for fifty years. Tomorrow I would have been free!"[1]

One of the single men I spoke with while doing research for my workshop presentation said he was not ready to get married because he was still having fun. When I asked him what he meant by this, he said he was not ready to give up his freedom. He told me that one of his brothers and a few friends who are married had echoed this sentiment to him. They agreed that after they got married their wives stopped being the "fun girlfriend" they used to be. This particular gentleman has an elder brother who got married three years earlier, and some of his apprehensions stem from what he has observed of that new marriage. I asked other single guys if they identified with this "marriage isn't fun" notion, and many did, but some did say they believe any relationship is as fun or exciting as you choose to make it.

I understand when single people view marriage as the "no-fun zone." The prevailing notion advertised or depicted in sitcoms and movies has really done a number on the average person's view of marriage. The image I typically see is the fumbling husband who is entirely clueless about the needs and desires of his lady. His wife is constantly disappointed by the lack of effort he makes to be affectionate, romantic, or even remotely interested. She is depicted as a shell of her former self who has settled for marriage. She spends her evenings slaving away for her family while

---

[1] Anne Jasiekiewicz, *A Laugh a Day: Jokes to Keep the Doctor Away.* (Bloomington, IN: AuthorHouse, 2010).

passively comparing herself to other women who seem more fulfilled. This picture would not be complete without mentioning that their sex life is nonexistent. To be fair, I have seen a few TV marriages that looked appealing. But these couples were usually super rich, and their money afforded them enough time and space to get away from one another once in a while.

When I got married and my social circle changed because of my new marital status, age, and career, I noticed how flawed this image of the "average married couple" was. True, there were couples who barely spoke to one another in public—the ones whose expressions looked like something out of *The Walking Dead*. But I also noticed the ones who took selfies together. Or sat on a park bench and fed the birds together. And the ones who jogged around the neighborhood at 5:45 a.m. every Saturday morning. Both kinds of marriages and every variation in between exist. This is one reason I'm excited about the value *For Better*, our free online marriage video library, provides: it presents a more balanced picture of these unions. I want you, whether single, married, divorced, or unsure, to interact with *For Better* and see couples who are taking it a day at a time just like you. Their stories are nuanced, rich and wonderful, just like yours. They do not live in the spotlight. They pay their bills or struggle to pay them. They were high school sweethearts or came together through an arranged marriage. My goal in providing you with a wide variety of real-life love stories in this book and at *For Better* is to dispel the lie that marriage is boring and devoid of adventure.

One such story I would like to share with you is that of *Lilian and Emeka*. When I met Lilian in our early twenties at York University, she enjoyed spending time with her girlfriends and attending the occasional party when work and school schedules permitted. She has a warmth about her, and a clever and entertaining sense of humor. We can spend hours laughing about absolute nonsense, and I love it! When she met Emeka he was doing his residency program to become a doctor. Since getting married, they have traveled more as a couple than they had in their single years. In less than a decade, they have had two beautiful children, are excelling in their various careers, and have travelled as a family to Australia, Africa, Europe, South America, and North America several times. They enjoy hosting parties and other get-togethers at home, and they are both having a blast in this new phase of their lives. They are a fun-loving couple who are always open to an adventure. Please pause in your reading and see their story on *For Better,* our free online marriage video library.

I always say marriage will be the longest, wealthiest, and wisest portion of your time on earth—enjoy every bit of it.

What I find remarkable about marriage is that even those who did not get it right the first time are still eager to give it a second and third try. Not bad for a boring institution, huh? As many as 60 percent of divorced women and men will marry again, many within just five years. There has to be something inherently special about marriage causing those who failed the first time to get up, dust themselves off, and try again.

If when finding a mate, you are blessed to find someone with a similar thirst for thrills, you can plan and create a lifetime of adventures. You can choose to stay on the conservative side and plan to do something out of the ordinary once a year or be more daring and shoot for weekly escapades. Your only limitation when it comes to having a fun marriage is your imagination. You can make lasting memories on a shoestring budget!

I'm a huge proponent for building life experiences, especially when you are young. But I lean more toward value-added experiences such as travel, learning a craft, experiencing different cultures, or exploring business opportunities before finding a life partner. I believe there is so much this beautiful world has to offer, although depending on your career and life's everyday demands, you may not get the chance to experience globetrotting just yet. While being young is the best time to build your portfolio and acquire experiences that are fascinating conversation starters and a great social currency, racking up sexual partners does not translate easily into the professional or relationship world. If you happen to be dating or courting when you are young, use this time to discover and explore your partner's important qualities, such as work ethic, credit score, religious beliefs, hobbies, and future ambitions, and see if they are congruent with yours. Capitalizing on the luxury of time you have in your youth gives you the luxury of choice in your later years. Make your twenties and thirties count!

I suggest leaving sexual exploration until marriage—if you do so, you minimize the chances of sordid details ending up where they should not, and harming your reputation because a scorned ex decided to share those details with others. Being in a healthy marriage means you have someone who is truly your partner and has seen you at your worst. If you cannot share your deepest secrets with him or her, who can you share them with? I propose you can have the most thrilling sex life while married because you can enjoy yourself with no inhibitions. Let it all hang out!

I have traveled, discovered more of myself, and gained immeasurably more exciting experiences in my first ten years of marriage than in my previous twenty-four years—and I'm just getting started! My husband and I put great effort into making each other enjoy our time on earth. He takes time to plan relaxing spa days or full-blown mom-cations for me and I do the same for him (minus the mom-cations). Because travel is a venture we both enjoy, we invest time and money in racking up those experiences.

After I gave birth to our second child, DiorRose, I was different. I did not have the same high energy and enthusiasm for my husband, life or ministry as I usually do—and he saw it. He began setting some money aside and convinced his best friend in Norway (we were living there at that time) to do the same for his wife. He planned an all-inclusive surprise mom-cation for me and his best friend's wife (I was the only one not aware of the surprise). On Christmas day that year, I was dumbfounded when I opened a small gift box with the website details, including airport pick up and drop off information. For his thirtieth birthday, I planned and raised funds from friends, family, and colleagues to send my amazing man to Japan. He loved it!

We also have our own set of close friends we enjoy spending time with. For instance, David and his close friends in North America have on occasion chosen a city and gone off on a boys' trip for a few days—a tradition I may copy soon.

We both made and make conscious decisions to enjoy our marriage. Besides treating each other on special occasions to solo trips, we have a blast and build memories as a family. As a family, we have experienced long distance road trips, skydiving, international travel, jet skiing, canoeing, and countless other activities. And since we are both foodies, we get a kick out of trying new cuisines together. I can only imagine the many more thrills we will rack up as we grow as a couple.

LILY B. DONKOR

Biblical Insight

One of the greatest rewards that come from being a minister or a minister's wife in my case, is the privilege to share in the very personal and at times private milestones of others. When young adults get a university acceptance letter, their parents call their pastor with the exciting news. When a long-time fiancé finally proposes, I get the text with an accompanying selfie and the ring zealously displayed. We have often been on the other side of the door when a team of doctors and nurses usher a new baby into the world. My husband has read from Psalms 90:12 many times while I attempt to comfort a grieving family member. This Bible passage says

*'So teach us to number our days,
That we may gain a heart of wisdom.'*

Attending a funeral is always a sobering experience. One cannot help but think about how tomorrow is not promised to our loved ones—in fact, our next breath is not guaranteed. To me, this text is not morbid but it instead invites me to probe more intently at my life. I like the wording of the New English Translation(NET). It reads:

*'So teach us to consider our mortality, [a]
so that we might live wisely. [b]'*

Considering my mortality means I ought to enjoy every waking moment. It means I should seize the opportunity to have fun with friends and family; go on that date and see where things lead; get started on the passion project I have been putting off. It also means since my life is finite,

MY FRUIT IS MAGICAL

I need to act wisely to get the best outcomes at various phases in my life. The small decisions I make daily, weekly, and yearly will culminate into a lifetime. This passage encourages me to live wisely so that I will be pleased with the totality of my life. My hope for you is that you will look back at your life in a few decades and be pleased with the overall outcome.

Having fun now does not need to cost you dearly in the future. Consider your tomorrow as you are making fun plans today.

Lasting Love Notes:

1. While you are young and single, map out what you want the rest of your life to look like. Then plan, work, and make decisions that bring you closer to that reality.

2. Getting married never has to mean the end of fun. In fact, it is an opportunity to build richer memories of adventures with your spouse, and to share them with your children.

3. Your twenties are the ideal time to build experiences that will build your wealth in the real world. Plus, you can regale others with the wealth of experiences you have acquired.

I cannot overemphasize the limitless fun you can have as a couple. So, go ahead and ditch the myth that you have to rack up all the fun stuff before you say, "I do." When it comes to having a fun-filled union, you are limited only by your imagination.

CHAPTER 2
He Has to Like Me for What's on the Inside First

Most of the time, an *attractive*, intelligent, witty, and kind lady who can cook will get the guy over an intelligent, witty, and kind lady who can cook. Everyone is attracted by what is attractive to them. Period.

> A man approached a very beautiful woman in a large supermarket and asked, "You know, I've lost my wife here in the supermarket. Can you talk to me for a couple of minutes?" "Why?" "Because every time I talk to a beautiful woman my wife appears out of nowhere."[2]

I love to celebrate women when they own and flaunt their individuality

---

2   Anne Jasiekiewicz, *A Laugh a Day: Jokes to Keep the Doctor Away*. (Bloomington, IN: AuthorHouse, 2010).

and quirks. All women are beautiful and unique, and house such wonderful treasures in their minds, bodies, and souls. Maybe you are confused about where this is all leading but hang on... I'm going somewhere with this. But first, let me tell you about Sheila.

A Coupling Narrative

I met Sheila when she was twenty-seven years old. She had just begun her graduate studies. She owned a rental property in the city where she attended university and lived in another home in a different city where she worked.

She grew up in a healthy and happy home. She is the only child to parents Clair and Gael, who have been married for thirty-one years.

Growing up, Sheila was not your stereotypical spoiled and bratty only child. She loved to hang out with Mom and help out whenever possible and often helped her elderly neighbor with yard work when she was not bogged down by schoolwork or chores.

Her mother is her role model; both parents are, actually. Her mother married her dad when she was twenty-four, two years after they met at a social event. Clair was gorgeous at five foot seven, with a slim build, a curvy waist, and a thirty-two-inch bust. That evening she had her shoulder-length hair in loose curls that had taken her forty-five minutes to achieve. She wore an A-line knee-length floral dress with spaghetti straps, accented by a chiffon white scarf tied in a bow around her neck. She wore sultry four-inch heels that elongated her already fabulous legs,

legs that Gael would rave about every time he spoke about Clair to his buddies. (I have had dinner with Sheila's family a few times and asked Gael and Clair my usual "How did you meet?" question.) Gael loved Clair from the inside out—every inch of her. And there was no doubt he walked a little taller whenever he had her on his arm.

Clair enjoyed being the part-time receptionist to a museum curator in the early years of their marriage. It allowed her to continue training and running long-distance marathons a few times a year. She kept up with running even after Sheila was born and started school.

On Sheila's sixth birthday, Clair and the other mothers exchanged stories of life, love, accomplishments, and perceived shortfalls. When the party was over, she left feeling deflated and painfully short on accomplishments. After leaving the receptionist job almost five years earlier, she had not bothered to rejoin the workforce—she saw no need, as Gael made more than enough to provide a comfortable life for the family.

After the birthday party, Clair returned to school and got her paralegal degree. Once she began working in the field, the long hours and mounds of endless research and paperwork did not bother her one bit—she was elated to be an empowered working woman. She no longer ran marathons, had not seen her regular hairdresser in ages, and the latest trends in *Cosmopolitan* made her stomach churn with regret. The magazine reminded her of her youthful years, the years she had spent grooming and tweaking and caring about what others thought about her.

Clair would automatically deride ladies who seemed to care

too much about their appearance, and Sheila picked up on it every time. She saw her mom as a vivacious, intelligent, loving mother who cared for and was loved by her father.

Sheila never gave a second thought to her own appearance. Her motto for getting dressed was "Pick up the clean one on the way out." She shared her mother's new ideology on beauty and aesthetics (or lack thereof) even though she had seen the pictures of mom all dolled up. As far as she was concerned, the beauty and cosmetics industry were one of the biggest scams, transforming women into liars and men into complicit victims.

Sheila had convinced herself that any man who did not want her for her appealing personality, zeal for life, and adventurous nature was not worth having. The last time we had lunch together, I asked her about her love life—which I tend to do with many of my friends, family, and acquaintances. Sheila was in one of the various phases of finding the one. Although she refused to admit it, she was heartbroken. Her former best friend, Scott, asked her to set him up with one of her "cute friends." Sheila has been crushing on Scott for as long as she could remember. They did everything together. They got along so well! She knew they were not a couple, but she thought he valued her more than the "dolled-up" girls she caught him staring at. Based on what she told me, I suggested because he was not attracted to her romantically from the start, he was resigned to being just her friend, which is not unheard of. She agreed with me but still did not see the need to alter her appearance. Out of pure duty, she then introduced him to her friend and decided he was not worthy of having her in his life—even as a friend.

MY FRUIT IS MAGICAL

The first time my husband saw me, he was attracted to my beaming smile and my then athletic physique, although he later told me he was also impressed by the way I spoke and carried myself. As time passed and we got to know each other on a deeper level, he still loved my beaming smile and my not-so-athletic shape, but he got the opportunity to uncover the many layers and facets of who I am. My physical appearance invited him, but he stayed for Lily the person. Unless your vision is obscured or you are blindfolded, your first impressions will always be informed by your sight. Most people looking to acquire a new home do not disregard the outer appearance and insist the inside of the property is the only element that matters in their decision-making process. Granted, the location, structure of the home, the floor plan, the plumbing, wiring, and overall feel of the interior are prime factors to consider before signing on the dotted line, but curb appeal or the lack of, it cannot be completely ignored. The same principle holds true for people.

The research I conducted for "Where Are All the Good Men?"—the talk I gave at the women's conference, had three components, one of which was an online anonymous survey. The survey consisted of poll and open-ended questions that solicited lengthier responses. One question asked participants to rate how critical a woman's physical appearance is in the decision to initiate a romantic relationship using a scale of one to five (with five being very important). Seventy-eight percent indicated a four or higher. In the follow-up question, some explained that appearance is not the primary factor in making a long-term relationship decision, but it plays a role in the initial stages. They have to be physically attracted to make the initial approach. A popular saying has it that women are moved by what they hear, and men are moved by what they see—that is why men lie, and women wear makeup. The reason we dress up for an interview is

35

because appearance matters. Neither you nor the interviewer is under the impression that your clothes or nicely groomed hair would be responsible for the brilliant ideas needed to get the job done, yet you put in an effort to present your best self. The same concept applies to meeting a potential spouse. Neither one of you is under the delusion that groomed hair, a Colgate smile, and a pushup bra are the keys to a successful marriage, but everyone appreciates a little window dressing.

In paying attention to your physical appearance, you enhance the complete package that you are. As humans, we interact with the world around us through our senses. Our experiences with people, places, and objects are never just one-dimensional. If you get the opportunity to interact with a potential spouse, how you engage his senses in the initial meeting will help determine the course the relationship takes. Although you should maintain his interest intellectually and emotionally, it does not hurt if he smiles every time he sees your beautiful smile or remembers how gorgeous you looked the first time he saw you or drifts briefly when a sweet aroma reminds him of your perfume.

Making yourself attractive has less to do with makeup and more to do with the psychology of how you present yourself to the world. Having spent the time to develop yourself, gain depth of character, and broaden your experiences, you simply promote your value when investing in your outward appearance.

I remember an episode of *The Cosby Show* when Vanessa Huxtable brought home her fiancé for the first time to meet her parents. She had been dating him for quite a while and finally brought him home one day and said, "mom, dad, this is my fiancé." She had not done Dabnis, the fiancé, justice when introducing him to her parents. When Dabnis spent the entire day with Clair and Cliff Huxtable, Vanessa's parents, they realized what a gem of a person their daughter had found. He was an industrious business owner, loved their daughter deeply, and respected the institution of marriage and family. When Cliff finally spoke to his daughter at the end of the evening, he chided her for doing her fiancé a disservice in the way she presented him to the family. He then asked Dabnis what his favorite food was, to which he responded, "Delicious porterhouse steak (no white lines) with crispy potatoes and sautéed mushrooms." Cliff encouraged him to picture it, to smell that decadent and expensive meal being presented to him. Then he said, "Now imagine I don't present it to you on a plate, but instead, I turn over the lid of a garbage can and I put your steak, your potatoes, and your mushrooms on it. Not too appetizing, is it? It is all in the presentation. That is the way she brought you here." Do not ignore your presentation. How you present yourself to others plays a role in how they perceive you—and potentially, how they treat you.

There are countless good-looking women of various shapes and colors from diverse socioeconomic backgrounds with a multitude of wonderful personality traits. Before a man gets the pleasure of speaking with you and learning of your many "write home to mama" qualities, he has to be *attracted* to you first. The other two or three women he is considering beside you may have nothing to offer but the pleasant smiles on their faces. You, on the other hand—as superb as you are—look as if you are pissed off all the time, and with your unwashed flannels and unkempt tresses, dressed to dig a ditch. Since your impressive résumé is not pasted on your face, your frown and disheveled appearance become your résumé. He will make a split-second decision based on what you have presented to him. This is where some might say, "Don't judge a book by its cover," to which I respond, ***If you have ever bought a book, you most likely first judged it by its cover—unless of course it came highly*** *recommended.* For those of us whose spouses did not get the five-star review of us from others before we met, it was our physical appearance that made the first impression.

Biblical Insight

But the Lord said to Samuel, 'Do not consider his appearance or his height, for I have rejected him. The Lord does not look at the things people look at. People look at the outward appearance, but the Lord looks at the heart.'

1 SAMUEL 16:7 NEW INTERNATIONAL VERSION – UK (NIV)

I have heard this passage of the Old Testament Bible used in many cases to chastise Christians, men in particular, who are seen to be too impressed by physical appearance. The passage is weaponized to shame them for admiring a woman's physical beauty. This verse in context has nothing to do with policing the male gaze or any gaze. This is not to say we should not practice self-control and respect for other people's bodies—we absolutely should, and there are dozens of other verses that say exactly that. This passage is simply stating a fact. It is stating the fact that it is impossible for you and I to see a person's motives or intentions: only God can see that. Only God can see from the onset if a suitor has evil intentions. It is through prayer, reading the Bible, God's words, and wise counsel that we can make the best decision—possibly, the one God intended for us to see.

God sent Samuel to Jesse's house to anoint one of Jesse's sons as the next King of Israel. Upon arriving, Samuel set eyes on Jesse's seven impressive looking sons with their warrior like statures. He was most impressed with Eliab and lifted up the horn of oil to anoint him when this famed passage occurred. Like any mortal, Samuel made a determination based on physical appearance and was ready to act on it. We make decisions every day based on what we see with our eyes and process in our brains. We decide on what to wear, which table to sit at, at a restaurant (when given the option), which car to buy, which shops to walk into, and so forth. Therefore, unless God himself speaks audibly to your would-be suitor; he will look at your outward appearance before he gets to know your heart.

Even the good book that lauds the virtues of having a noble and upright character does not neglect putting a value on outward appearance. Unless you only plan to be attractive to God, it is profitable (not just for your love life) to present well to the world around you.

Lasting Love Notes:

1. Men do place value on a woman's physical appearance.

2. Take ownership of people's first impressions of you and the image you project to the outside world.

3. Engaging a potential spouse's interest on multiple levels is valuable.

This is not an endorsement of spending excessively on your clothing, piling on the makeup, and adorning your face with a plastic smile in the pursuit of love. What I am suggesting is that you take ownership of your first, second, and third impressions on people. Appearances do matter, so give Mr. May-be-right the opportunity to get to say, "Hey, you wanna grab some coffee?" and to see you as relationship material rather than just a friend.

CHAPTER 3
He Must Be Able to Provide for Me

I am as old-fashioned as the next person when it comes to relationships. I like my man to open doors for me, write me sentimental notes even when it is not a special occasion, and take the lead. When David opens a jar I cannot seem to loosen, I still blush a little. I like hugging him at the door when he gets in (whenever I happen to be home) and asking how his day was.

I love the idea of taking care of my husband and our three children. I enjoy crafting and picking out clothes for them. I occasionally enjoy cooking and trying out a new recipe, but I mostly do it so we do not starve. I also embrace the concept of my man taking care of me financially. But as much as I love being the matron of my mansion, all the doting, cleaning, and catering typically happens between 6:00 p.m. and 11:00 p.m., after I have finished working for the day.

> It is 1957, and Bobby goes to pick up his date, Peggy Sue. Peggy Sue's father answers the door and invites him in. He asks Bobby what they're planning to do on the date. Bobby politely responds that they'll probably just go to the malt shop or to a drive-in movie. Peggy Sue's father suggests, "Why don't you kids go out and screw? I hear all of the kids are doing it." Bobby is shocked. "Excuse me, sir?" "Oh yes, Peggy Sue really likes to screw. She'll screw all night if we let her." Peggy Sue comes downstairs and announces that she's ready to go. About 20 minutes later, a thoroughly disheveled Peggy Sue rushes back into the house, slams the door behind her, and screams at her father, "Dad! The Twist! It's called the Twist!"[3]

My values may be old-fashioned, but my financial demands are as modern as they get. Gone are the days when the man was the primary or sole breadwinner and his income was enough to provide for the family. I have a full-time job to help pay the bills because I understand we have to use our combined resources to attain the lifestyle we both enjoy.

I was raised in a single-parent home by my father. He worked hard to provide all our necessities and at times allowed us to indulge in some extravagances at his expense. I recall being in the tenth grade and seeing an acting lessons poster at the bus stop. In less than two minutes, I imagined I would get the best theatrical training, be ahead of my peers in the class, and be singled out by our acting coach. Then my agent would land me a role in a midsize production downtown, where someone important

---

[3] Frank Verano, *All Kinds of Humor: Jokes, Quips, and Fun Stuff for Many Occasions over Forty Categories Book II.* (Self-published, Xlibris Corporation, 2012.)

would see my incredible natural talent and range. They would immediately cast me alongside an A-list celebrity, and I would be well on my way to fulfilling my dream of being a mild-mannered public figure who had never lost touch with her humble beginnings yet enjoyed the finer things in life. (And I know I am not the only one who has had that daydream.) here and then, I ripped the poster off the bus shelter in the hopes Daddy would not crush my dreams by saying no to the $580 fee for a three-day course. I got home and told him all about my day and how well I had done on my test, exaggerating my mark a little to butter him up, before asking for permission and the money to follow my pipe dream.

To make a long story short, by the end of the following week, I had attended only two of the three classes (because I could not foresee stardom by going to the third class). I did not have an agent, but I now had my first part-time job to pay back my $580 loan. As much as my father took pride in being a provider and encouraged most of my dreams and innumerable under baked "passions," the reality remained that life required money. And someone has to pick up the tab. It is vital to understand that no matter how passionate you are about your life; it is not anyone's obligation to finance it. Nothing drove this concept home for me more than Dad's one-liner (in his Edo-Nigerian accent): "There is no free lunch in America." He made sure I understood that you work for what you get, and you get what you work for. I am grateful he left me with this lesson before he passed away.

Ladies (and gentlemen for that matter), be willing and able to pay the toll for the life you want. You can do so in any number of ways. It may be that you and your partner decide he should stay home with the kids, and you will use your higher earning potential outside the home. Or it can mean you both work, but one of you works part-time and takes care of an ailing family member. Whatever the scenario, it is best if you do not seek out mates based primarily on their ability to provide for you. Linda's story is an example of why you might be doing yourself a disservice by clinging to the myth that a man should support you financially.

A Coupling Narrative

The first time I saw Linda was at a friend's wedding; it was an intimate reception with roughly sixty in attendance. She sang a breathtaking tribute to the newlyweds, getting a standing ovation, and moving many guests to tears. When dinner and the formal part of the reception had ended, I made my way over to congratulate her on a wonderful performance. We discovered we had a few mutual friends and had crossed paths several times before. We exchanged pleasantries and both introduced the other to mutual friends we had come to the reception with. Later, four of the five of us convened on a furnished patio at the reception venue—it was a gorgeous evening and a few people were mingling and having drinks outside as well.

Linda, Maria, Stacey, and I shared how much we were enjoying the wedding reception after a quaint marriage ceremony at the groom's church. We overheard two guys behind us, one of whom was saying he had moved back in with his parents temporarily until he could get back on his feet. From the little we heard, he no longer liked working as a financial analyst and wanted to earn a living pursuing his passion, photography. This got us talking about our own passions and whether any of us were actually earning a living doing what we loved.

MY FRUIT IS MAGICAL

Maria and Stacey were both nurses, and Stacey said she had always wanted to be a nurse and doing so for the past seven years had been entirely fulfilling. Maria was satisfied with her nursing career too, although she enjoyed her income more than the actual work. Overall, she too, was content. She was passionate about hiking, and nursing afforded her and her husband, a personal trainer, the means to travel to a desired hiking trail at least once a year. I shared I was perfectly happy working as an executive assistant at a tech company, but I would not call it a passion of mine (I have since moved from that company and country but one of my many roles is still working as an Executive Assistant at a non-profit). It was a career I enjoyed and was good at. Before Linda shared her occupation with us, she asked if Maria and I were working out of a sense of obligation since we were not passionate about our careers. Our responses were similar: we both gained satisfaction from our work, we had outlets to explore our passions, and we worked to help sustain our families and lifestyles. Our answers did not exactly impress her.

Linda had decided the only way to truly enjoy her life was to pursue her passion full-time. She had worked as a purchasing officer for a major clothing retail chain for three years. She earned a decent salary and the bonuses were nothing to scoff at, but she was increasingly unhappy. She mentioned to her live-in boyfriend, Mark, she wanted to sing full-time, but they did not discuss the logistics and financial implications of her decision before she quit her job. Linda's hasty move and her boyfriend's increased expenses began putting a strain on their relationship. It bothered her that he was not supporting her "difficult yet bold" decision, and he was disappointed and frustrated by her inconsiderate behavior. Linda felt he should have looked at the big picture and been able to shoulder the financial challenge like a man. She felt she was not a needy or dependent person, but if she needed her man to take care of her at any point that it should not have been a problem. She had lost respect for Mark and figured if a man could not be depended on during a transitional period, he really was not worth her time. She was not necessarily looking for a rich man—just one who earned enough to take care of his woman's needs. She broke up with Mark, moved out of their apartment, and rented a room with two other ladies.

This wedding was not Linda's first paid singing gig. She had performed at other weddings, birthday celebrations, and a few corporate events while working as a purchasing officer. Now she figures since she is going to give it her all full-time, she can dedicate herself completely to her craft and earn more money. She's had a few dates since Mark, but none of the men were marriage material, and she refuses to settle for a man who cannot take care of "his family." Although she still plans on sticking to finding a man with the financial buoyancy to support her lifestyle, she admits she has had some less than desirable encounters along the way. She met and dated a dentist for a few months and desperately tried to make it work, but she could not get past what a complete bore he was. Their conversations mostly revolved around the weather and when her next singing gig would be (on average she performed twice a month). The other prospects simply have yet to buy into her philosophy.

MY FRUIT IS MAGICAL

An article was published in the *New York Times* highlighting the realities of today's economy on the average millennial household. It pointed out that even though a heterosexual couple is earning more now than in previous generations, the spending power is not as strong. Both parties are obliged to work longer hours to be able to afford what generations before them did.

> "The gains in income were also driven by increased employment, rather than increased pay. The average annual earnings of both male and female full-time workers actually declined last year."[4]

Women, in particular, are the cause of the increased income. The Pew Research states "The growth in household incomes among young adults has been driven in part by Millennial women, who are working more—and being paid more—than young women were in previous years."[5]

Gone are the days when a single income provided a comfortable life for the average American family. I do not blame you for wanting to secure your financial future. In fact, I commend you for taking this aspect of your married life very seriously. Far too many people are not conscientious about mapping out where they need to be financially in five, ten, or thirty years. So, kudos to you! But please remember, what works for you also works for men. Men also know what it takes in today's economy to raise 2.5 children, pay for the ballooning costs of education, and have a healthy work-life balance while maintaining their financial freedom. Just like

---

[4] Binyamin Appelbaum and Robert Pear, "U.S. Household Income Rises to Pre-Recession Levels, Prompting Cheers and Questions," *New York Times*, Sept. 12, 2018

[5] Richard Fry, "Young adult households are earning more than most older Americans did at the same age," Pew Research Center, Dec. 11, 2018.

you, he does not want to "just get by" or struggle to make ends meet. He also wants to thrive! A responsible man will assess his capabilities, plot a course for his future, and partner with someone he is confident can help him realize his goals. It may very well be that he prefers his wife not to have to work—she can crochet all day or teach a watercolor class. Or he may deem it necessary to marry a woman who will make less, the same, or more than him. It is his prerogative.

The question is if you choose him for financial security, will he choose you for the same reason? In that event, instead of looking for a mate primarily for his financial strength, why not strengthen yourself financially? That way, you enter a new relationship from a position of strength and not desperation; a position where money does not matter quite as much. It means you can look past his menial job and strike up a conversation. It means you may not snub men who seem unlikely to meet your financial needs. I would hate for you to find yourself in a desperate position where love and attraction are not primary factors in looking for a spouse. In the words of the French philosopher and historian, Voltaire, "Don't think money does everything or you are going to end up doing everything for money." There are intrinsic qualities that are necessary for a fulfilling relationship that money simply cannot buy.

You may decide you will only consider men who are able and willing to provide for you, and that is perfectly fine. But men also have the right to search for women based on their financial position and potential. Also, keep in mind what stage of life you and your prospects are in. Consider the opportunity costs he may be paying. For example, he may be working a part-time janitorial job now to pay for schooling to enable him to earn more in five years. Or, just like you, he may be working hard to achieve his set goal and cannot afford eating out more than twice a month. What I am saying is, it may not be judicious to estimate a man's long-term ability to provide based on his earnings in his twenties and thirties. By focusing primarily on money, you deny yourself the opportunity to meet men who are "wealthy" in other areas.

My earlier research found that many men are not necessarily against a man providing for his family. Most were willing to be the primary or only breadwinner if able to do so. Their concern was why a woman would require such support. Was she not capable of earning a living? Did she have some sort of disability that prevented her from working? Did her own financial irresponsibility cause her to have to rely on someone else? Having to consider whether a woman has had a setback preventing her from caring for herself as a fully functional adult gave these men pause. ence, if you make it known that a man must be able to provide for you, you may be doing yourself a disservice by discouraging potential mates.

Building your own credit profile strengthens your skill set and safeguards you in case of life's eventualities. In my role in the church, I'm saddened when an elderly woman loses her lifelong partner after decades together. It is even more heartbreaking to witness her struggling to learn the value of his estate. Even more troubling is when such financial crises occur earlier in life—for example when a woman who depended on her spouse financially learns he's lost his job or they separate. These sudden changes in family life are enough to rattle anyone, but it is far worse when you have little to no financial stability outside of your spouse.

Studies show that women outlive men, yet women have fewer assets at retirement and far fewer in old age. Numerous factors are at play here, not least of which is a lack of intent to build your own financial profile.

I challenge you to recognize and unleash your earning potential. Dig deep to find your marketable skills and passions, and get any needed training to develop those skills. Give yourself the opportunity to find out what you are really made of, and see how your brain power translates to earning power. Even if you do not end up owning a private jet, you will know you have value. And understanding your value will give you the freedom and confidence to find a partner who tickles your fancy.

Biblical Insight

"The one who works his land
will have plenty of food,
but whoever chases fantasies
will have his fill of poverty."

PROVERBS 28:19 (CSB)

The first two lines of this verse are empowering. It gives the reader, any reader, the assurance that you are certain of success if you apply yourself. And I will echo that sentiment. You will have what you need if YOU work for it. There is always a possibility you can get what others work for but that is as certain as someone letting me cut in the checkout line at a grocery store. It could happen. Or they could rightfully scoff at my attempts and send me to the back of the line. I would rather go for the sure thing and save myself some embarrassment, would you not, too?

There is a measure of pride and personal responsibility adults need to have to be fully functioning members of society. It makes for better communities, neighborhoods and certainly, marriages. Knowing that you can rely on your partner to be resourceful (not just financially) is a great feeling. Be that resourceful partner!

The second part of the verse says, 'whoever chases fantasies will have his fill of poverty.' In rereading this bible verse I'm reminded of the fact that the overwhelming majority of lottery winners end up broke within a few years of hitting the jackpot. Without the character, knowledge and work ethic needed to acquire wealth, the fantasy of being rich always remains a fantasy. I do not know anyone who wishes to struggle financially for their entire life. We all aspire to have at least enough to live comfortable lives and this verse in Psalms teaches us exactly what to do and what NOT to do, to achieve that. We are all trying to figure out this thing called life for the first time. It can be overwhelming at times. Ask for help. There is a plethora of free apps, videos, and resource centers that are designed specifically for those of us who entered adulthood with little to no financial literacy. And that ignorance at times can cause you to seek out a partner to carry that undesired weight.

I challenge you to take the words of Proverbs 28:19 to heart. Let it change your mindset about how you relate to your finances. You can write it out and place it in a visible place as a frequent reminder that you alone are in charge of your financial future. A partner can come along to support by adding to your knowledge and helping with the plans you already have about your money. I venture to guess it would take some work, time, and skills to plot how to get attached to someone who has means. I encourage you to put that same effort into becoming a person who has enough for themselves and more to give.

LILY B. DONKOR

Lasting Love Notes:

1. It is a great idea to consider the financial implications of marriage. However, your own hard work and fiscal practices are a better basis for a financially secure future than marriage.

2. Avoid eliminating potentially goodsuitors based on their financial status in their twenties and even early thirties. You run the risk of not factoring in their current opportunity costs.

3. Build your own financial and credit identity. It will build your sense of accomplishment and value as an individual. Your goal should be to complement, not depend on, your partner.

I remember a story I read about President and Mrs. Obama. Barack and Michelle had visited a local restaurant in Chicago, and someone mentioned to the president Michelle had dated the present owner of the establishment before they had met. The president looked at his wife with a smirk and said, "So if you'd married him, you would own half of this joint." Michelle smiled back at him and said, "If I'd married him, he would be the president of the United States of America." Michelle knows what she brings to the table.

I hope you do not narrow your search to include only men who can provide for you at this stage—you may end up passing up the opportunity to make your man a president!

CHAPTER 4
I Need to Be Established First

I have noticed the negative connotations around being a stay-at-home mom—so negative that some women are petrified at the thought of not having a career, substantial savings, and a house before they meet their **Mr. Right**. Being a stay-at-home mom is an extremely difficult and demanding job. I find that spending eight hours with my infant son at home is worlds more draining than spending ten hours at the office—although there are days when being at the office wipes me out. But overall, being a stay-at-home mom is a demanding profession in its own right. If stay-at-home moms were to charge based on market prices for every task they have performed in twenty-four hours, they would command a respectable annual salary.

That being said, some women would rather soar to the top of the corporate ladder or achieve their career ideals, which is commendable. In the framework of relationships, a desire to excel professionally does not necessarily have to result in a stagnant or nonexistent love life. You can achieve success in both career and love alongside each other.

I am a firm believer that love can find you at any age and any stage of life, even during your climb up the corporate ladder. However, finding love requires your openness to the possibility. If you have just graduated from college, go ahead and pursue that dream job until Mr. Right comes along. If you desire and are able to purchase a house, I say more power to you as you sign on that dotted line. Do not settle for the $30,000 car when you have budgeted for the $60,000 one just because your family thinks the higher price tag may intimidate men. I want you to take life by the horns, live out loud, and achieve to your highest potential. Do not cower to accommodate someone else's insecurities.

What I will caution you against is having static ultimatums for yourself, the kind that say: I *must* own my own home before I get married, I *must* have $30,000 in my savings account before I get engaged, or I *must* be made a partner at the firm before I entertain the idea of a serious relationship.

I have to admit, I was guilty of placing these demands on myself for a period in my life. After earning my bachelor's degree, I, like most university graduates in North America, was laden with tuition debt. I told myself I had to pay it all off before I got married to prevent burdening someone else with this responsibility. I worked a full-time job while in school and a full-time job after graduating, plus I earned extra income as a hairdresser, all with a single goal in mind—get rid of that loan. When my now husband and I began dating, one of the many questions he asked me was when I planned to get married. I did not necessarily have an age in mind, but I told him I would be ready when the right person came along, and after I had paid off my student loan.

MY FRUIT IS MAGICAL

I believe he already knew then he wanted to marry me; hence he began a line of questioning that caused me to examine my ultimatum while not imposing his opinion (he is very good at this). He asked how much I had left to pay off, how much the interest rate was, how much I had paid so far, how much I was making now, how much I would potentially earn in the next two to four years, and so forth. I also factored in the reality of having to pay for rent, utilities, groceries, transportation, etc. At the rate I was going, I would be eligible for marriage at forty-two. Forty-two might be ideal for some, but not for me. Besides, there was absolutely no reason why I could not continue paying down my debt while I was married (as long as my potential partner was in agreement).

In retrospect, I realized I was so adamant about taking care of my debt because I did not want to seem like a liability. Although I knew I was talented, hardworking, great company, and had a substantial amount in savings and investments, I still felt David might think less of me because of my student loan. I never wanted to give anyone the satisfaction of thinking I owed them anything. I felt my debt would make me vulnerable to potential blame during marriage, especially since he did not have a student loan debt. I wanted him to know I could take care of myself and was not waiting for a savior.

I have come to realize there was a measure of pride and naïveté in my thinking. People enter business partnerships revealing their assets, debts, and liabilities, and it is up to both parties to assess whether the partnership would be mutually beneficial. If, as a business owner, you want to operate without loans before considering a venture that could increase your net worth, you might miss out on tremendous opportunities. A wiser course of action is to make a well-informed decision based on all the facts.

> A man is getting into the shower just as his wife is finishing up her shower when the doorbell rings. The wife quickly wraps herself in a towel and runs downstairs. When she opens the door, there stands Bob, the next-door neighbor. Before she says a word, Bob says, "I'll give you $800 to drop that towel." After thinking for a moment, the woman drops her towel and stands naked in front of Bob. After a few seconds, Bob hands her $800 and leaves. The woman wraps her up in the towel again and goes back upstairs. When she gets to the bathroom, her husband asks, "Who was that?" "It was Bob, the next-door neighbor," she replies. "Great," the husband says, "did he say anything about the $800 he owes me?"
>
> Moral of the story: If you share critical information pertaining to credit and risk with your shareholders (partner) in time, you may be in a position to prevent avoidable exposure.[6]

I had to realize I was exactly what David wanted and needed; student loan included. Besides, I had the rest of my life to build, learn, and achieve my fullest potential—I did not need to cap my timeline at two, five, or ten years. Some people may need only three years to achieve what they consider greatness, while others need a lifetime. If you need more time to accomplish your goals, denying yourself love or a relationship may be too costly. Consider what you could be missing. In my case, the level

---

6   Jack V. Grazi, *A Laugh A Day Will Keep the Doctor Away!* (Self-published, Xlibrix Corporation, 2010.)

of collaboration, encouragement, and support I get from David is absolutely invaluable. I am pretty sure he would not have waited until my forty-second birthday to pop the question—especially since that is still seven years away. He, my student loan, and I have been happily married for over ten years—with plans of divorcing the student loan sooner rather than later. But not everyone has followed my path. I want you to now read the experience of Ashley and Hank to see how static ultimatums shaped their relationship.

A Coupling Narrative

Ashley and Hank attended the same college and met in 2010 during their second year in a business undergraduate program. She was the quintessential girl next door, just as gorgeous with no makeup and a baseball cap as she was all dressed up. Hank and Ashley had mutual friends and ran into one another on occasion. The two became Facebook friends and checked on one another sometimes, but Hank always wanted more. He was completely infatuated with Ashley and really enjoyed her company—even if he had to do so in the midst of all their friends.

He decided to use Ashley's number for the first time and asked her to dinner on Valentine's Day. He would pick her up at 6:30 p.m., but the rest of the evening would be a surprise. Ashley got in his car, and off they went. She engaged him in small talk as she half-jokingly sent a text of his picture and license plate to her sister and best friend with instructions to call the police if they had not heard from her by midnight.

Ashely could tell how nervous Hank was. He was six foot five and ruggedly handsome with a crisp white smile. He should have oozed confidence, but instead, he was all nerves at the reality of sitting inches away from Ashley. After driving for a few minutes, he pulled into a strip mall and asked her to pick a color from among swatches of yellow, red, white, and purple.

"Purple," she said with a giggle.

He left the engine running and darted out of the car. Her heart fluttered because of the excitement she noticed in his eyes and the anticipation of what the night could bring.

"Be my valentine," he said, opening her passenger-side door and handing her a single long-stemmed purple rose.

"Of course."

That was Hank: a spontaneous gentleman whose sights were set on Ashley. They enjoyed one another's company, challenged each other mentally and emotionally, and had epic disagreements. And the physical attraction was palpable. They had been dating for a little over a year when graduation rolled around. Both families went out to dinner together to celebrate their academic achievements and to get to know one another officially, since Ashley and Hank were getting pretty serious.

Hank had intentionally waited until after graduation to begin hinting at the possibility of looking at rings before the end of the year; they had already agreed the relationship would lead to marriage.

Things became a tad uneasy between the two in the months following graduation. Ashley loved Hank and pictured a life with him but was adamant she had to be a few years into her career and buy a new car before entertaining marriage or wedding plans. She had a clear vision of how her life was supposed to play out: graduate, make a name for herself, get married, have three kids, and travel.

Hank told himself the arguments and disagreements could be avoided if he was not crazy about her. At least he could then have walked away because they could not see eye to eye. But he loved her and did not want to dissuade her from pursuing her vision for her life. Still, they argued because he did not understand why she could not accomplish her career goals in parallel with marriage, or why they could not wake up as husband and wife each morning, and unwind after work while encouraging and challenging each other to conquer the world as one. He did not want to date indefinitely; he wanted a commitment to merge and build their lives together as a family.

The tremendous friction in their relationship caused them to break up for a few months at a time. Ashley continued making gains in her career, and Hank was genuinely happy for her and celebrated a few of these gains. Meanwhile, he was racking up his own stellar accomplishments. At last, Ashley is ready to get married and start a life with Hank, but he is not as excited as he has been before, and he has dated a few girls while they were on a break—although nothing serious. He still loves Ashley but has become accustomed to spending little time with her. She is now ready for marriage: the third item on the vision board, while Hank needs a little time before revisiting the idea of marriage again.

The bedrock of any relationship is communication. Famed author and life coach Anthony Robbins said it like this: "To effectively communicate, we must realize that we are all different in the way we perceive the world and use this understanding as a guide to our communication with others." It is important for the other person to know your intentions, but more critically, especially when it comes to matters of the heart, your motivations. Let that person know what you need but also why you need it.

It was good for Ashley to share her career intentions with Hank, but she did not go far enough. Once they reached an impasse, it was time to communicate motives. Ashley could have lovingly explained to Hank why she believed having a solid career to stand on was a minimum requirement for marriage. She could have explained that she would feel vulnerable without a solid career; that although she loved and trusted him, she remembered how her aunt was left almost penniless, unable to provide for herself after a divorce. It is understandable why Ashley was apprehensive about entering a marriage without attaining her desired professional status, but her decision was motivated by fear. And that fear convinced her men could not be fully trusted to support women in pursuing their professional or financial goals.

Like Ashley, I also needed to recognize why I wanted to hold off on marriage. It was not that I did not feel I was ready to take my relationship to the next level. Nor did I think that David would mistreat me based on my financial profile at the beginning of the relationship. But like Ashley, I wanted to hold off until I was "secure." I hope you would not reject the chance to love and be loved while reaching for your goals. Experiencing love and building your career can be done in tandem. The key is to find a mate who supports you and encourages you to follow your passions and strive to achieve your aspirations. With your partner by your side, you might come to find you enjoy the unexpected detours life has a way of taking you on. If Ashley had shared her insecurity and her reason for drawing such a harsh line in the sand, it might have reassured Hank of her continued commitment to the relationship. From this point of transparency and acceptance, they could have then charted a course that would have addressed both of their desires while preserving their love story.

This is a good time to hop over to lovenyou.org and watch *Gary & Julie's* story. They were in a similar place over twenty-five years ago. Let us see how they handled it.

I hope you realize how immensely resourceful you are. Whether before or during a marriage, you must not let your capacity to achieve your goals be hindered by anyone. My husband and children have been a huge motivation for me to push and challenge myself. I am immensely excited by my future prospects, and it is wonderful talking it out daily with someone who has my best interests at heart.

Biblical Insight

"Many plans are in a person's mind,
but the Lord's purpose will succeed."

PROVERBS 19:21; COMMON ENGLISH BIBLE (CEB)

Before I met David, I had racked up a few tens of thousands of dollars in student loan debts. And like many people, I had made a working plan to pay it off. I would pay a fixed amount every month (hoping my income remained the same or increased) and eventually be rid of this burden. In a sense, I was consumed in my thoughts and emotions by this mountain of undesired debt. I was irritated that it was now part of my life and I wanted to do everything to get rid of it. I would have visceral reactions of shame when it came up in conversation. Simply put, it was not something I was proud of. That is the reason when David asked me when I planned to get married, among my top responses were, "when I pay off my student loan". I was that keen. I had mapped out a strict plan that left no room for anything that would slow down my progress; certainly, not costly socializing and dating.

I had my plans. But God had His purpose for me. What I have since realized in my core is that purpose is far greater than plans. And I must begin with the purpose in mind before mapping out my plan. This revelation has worked wonders for me and I invite you to try it. God had the overall purpose of why I am here on earth and the role that meeting and marrying David would play in my life.

I had a plan to pay off a big bill and move on to the next thing on my checklist. In implementing my plan, I could not see the forest from the trees. I was not looking at the bigger picture of my life. I was focused on this one thing and even used that as a reason to put off a potential husband. Clearly, getting married would not stop me from paying a bill but I was caught up on perception. How would a potential spouse view me? Would he see me as a liability? Would he use my debt as a point of attack during an argument in marriage? My pride had conjured up so many scenarios to convince me my debt placed me at a severe disadvantage and must be eliminated immediately. All this before I even met a guy. Is that not crazy?!

I am so glad I gave David the chance to show me how wrong I was. I would caution against what I was doing. I encourage you to make plans for your future at the stage you are at now. And rather than working with strict ultimatums, allow yourself room to readjust based on new information and circumstances you may not have planned for. Taking stock of my life's events, the truly meaningful ones happened when I allowed purpose to override my plan. In my early twenties, my plans were simply to finish with my first degree and get a job. But God's purpose for me in those trying years following my daddy's death was to share my pain and experience in the form of a gospel album. Today, my three-year-old daughter plays that CD over and over and over in the car and it warms my heart to hear her rapping all my lyrics. I planned to have a large family, settle in a quiet neighborhood, and live in our forever home by the time I turned thirty-five. Again, God's purpose for me has been quite different. David and I were transplanted to a different country with only a week's notice because of his profession. We have spent the past eight years travelling and living in different counties. We do not have the forever home yet, but I could not have planned a more fulfilling decade. I will share that very exciting story in a different book.

Go ahead and make plans, but allow life, and if you are a believer, allow God to work out His purpose for you.

Lasting Love Notes:

1. Love can find you at any stage in your climb to success. Be open to the possibilities and avoid static ultimatums. Trust yourself to choose a responsible partner who will have your best interests at heart.

2. Allow your decision to be financially secure before marriage

to be driven by pure motives and not by fear, pride, or another person's unfortunate outcome.

3. Rest assured you can grow and achieve personal and professional milestones while married. Countless couples around you have done it, and so can you.

One of my favorite Oprah Winfrey quotes is "Everyone wants to ride with you in the limo, but what you want is someone who will take the bus with you when the limo breaks down." I am confident my husband would ride the bus with me and we would have a great time doing it. Know that marriage never has to mean you have settled or given up on you. It is a partnership that can enrich your already promising future.

CHAPTER 5
My Fruit Is Magical

My son David II (named after my husband) was an early talker. He began forming entire sentences and communicating in clear, concise words well before he turned two. When we noticed he started repeating our words and expressions at seven months, my husband and I became very mindful of how we spoke and what we allowed him to be exposed to. We have always spoken to him in full sentences, as though we were speaking to someone who understood exactly what we were saying.

When he was seven months old, he spilled apple juice on himself. I carried him over to his changing table, undressed him, and proceeded to wipe him down with moist towelettes. As I wiped his fingers, I would say, "We are cleaning David's fingers." When I got to his chest, I said, "We are cleaning David's chest," and so forth. When I began cleaning his private parts, I paused because I had not yet decided what we would call them. Were we going with the anatomically correct term, "penis"? Or opting for a widely accepted euphemism like "pee pee," "wiener," or "winky"? I decided to split the difference and said, "We are cleaning David's man-parts." By the time you read this book he most likely will know and understand that the correct term is "penis," but coining that nickname then served us well. Now, for the purpose of this chapter, we are going to coin another term for our vagina, and that word is "fruit." From here on out I will only refer to our lady parts as fruit. You can decide what kind of fruit yours is.

As I mentioned earlier, most of the subject matter covered in this book was born of personal experiences, coaching women, or chatting with friends, colleagues, or strangers about relationships. This chapter is no different. Consider the story of one of my mentees, Betty.

I had just finished putting my son to sleep and was picking up his toys in the living room when I got a long-distance phone call from Betty. She was on the verge of making a few crucial relationship decisions and thought it would be a good idea to get my perspective. It is always a wise decision to seek the advice, or at least perspective, of someone you respect when making important life decisions. There is no need to tough it out on your own. The Book of Proverbs in the Bible puts it this way: "Where no counsel is, the people fall; but in the multitude of counselors there is safety".[7] It never hurts to ask!

Before we called it a night, Betty asked my opinion on a matter a friend of hers was facing, (she identified her as Serita, but admitted this was not her real name). Serita had decided she was only going to consider marrying a man who earned enough money to support both of them because she did not want to work. Before I could draw any conclusions, I asked Betty a few questions about what her friend thought she had to offer that could attract and keep the kind of man she was seeking.

---

7   *NKJV Hugs Bible for Women*, Thomas Nelson Inc., 2008.

MY FRUIT IS MAGICAL

Betty said with a chuckle, "She said all men want one thing, and she never disappoints."

Without much thought, I asked, "Is her fruit magical?"

After Betty and I had a good laugh, I felt obligated, even to myself, to unpack the thinking behind my rhetorical question.

I have colleagues with the most electrifying personalities. You would be enraptured by their charisma and warmth, yet they're not always successful in keeping the love of their lives, try as hard as they might. I know women who can rival Martha Stewart when it comes to their homemaking skills, but their husbands still left them. I know some ladies who are so physically attractive that other women question whether God is fair. These earthly goddesses have been cheated on and jilted by lovers. I have also had mentors who prayed and sought the face of their God and all His angels but could not get their men to stay. Yet here was this friend of Betty's who apparently did not have a pot to piss in but was touting her ability to have sex as the anchor for a sustained relationship. This alone was the source of her bold confidence in her man-getting and keeping abilities. And so the only logical question I had was, "Is her fruit magical?"

Would it provide a warmth comforting enough to make a man forget he had just lost his job? Would it be strong enough to hold the home together after he had lost his mom and spiraled into depression? Is it so fragile that he would devote every waking thought to how to protect and cherish it? Would it remain exotic and sensual enough to make his client who looks like a supermodel seem like chopped liver to him? Was her fruit magical? Let us explore this question further with more about Betty's friend, Serita.

LILY B. DONKOR

A Coupling Narrative

Serita was a tomboy with striking natural beauty in her teenage years. She dated the same boy for four years until she suddenly lost interest and broke up with him when she turned nineteen. He stalked her for a few months after she dumped him until she got a restraining order.

Following that relationship, Serita dated an amateur baseball player for three months during his training camp session in Boston. When he left town to try out for a team in California without telling her, she was devastated but found solace in the arms of one of his former teammates. Serita and Drew were inseparable, and although his teammates ridiculed him for taking his friend's leftovers, he was much too happy to care. Drew had originally planned to return to Texas after his second season but extended his stay an extra semester—primarily to be with Serita.

On one of their dates, Drew was feeling smitten and decided Serita deserved to know the complete truth about him. He told her he was married and had been for the past year and a half. He had come to Boston to play baseball two months after his wedding. He had imagined having just a fling with Serita but was now captivated by her and wanted to end his marriage. It took her a few days to get up from her bed after the shock, heartbreak, and anger she felt at what Drew had told her. But once those emotions subsided, Serita was feeling all sorts of confidence and was beside herself with joy. She already had to get a restraining order against one boyfriend, but this one was ready and willing to leave his new bride for her! If ever she had been self-assured and buoyant, it was then! Her ego had received such a boost that she began using her looks and sex appeal to get favors—not necessarily sleeping with the men, though. She decided to invest heavily in her clothes, shoes, and other adornments. She was convinced once she presented the right man with her assets, her future was as good as secured.

Since embarking on this new venture, she has landed herself a few dates and gifts, but Mr. Right is still elusive. Serita has not given up on her approach, but she is beginning to realize she may not be the only one getting dolled up and waiting for her prince to notice her. As she sits in fancy hotel lobbies, visits art galleries, and loiters through the men's section in Neiman Marcus, she notices other stunningly beautiful women dressed to impress as well. They also strut, swing their hair when they laugh, and perfectly apply the right amount of makeup to still look "natural." Irrespective of the perceived competition, Serita holds on to her truth about her power—the power to turn reasonable gentlemen into stalkers and adulterers. Serita is still certain that if she can get past the introductory stage of a relationship with a man and he earns the privilege to know the magic of her fruit, she can seal the deal. And so Serita waits.

Sex is a beautiful and pleasurable expression of love. But like gifts, dates, and goals, sex is not the only or even the main ingredient for an enjoyable, fulfilling marriage.

It has been said that "it's absolutely unfair for women to say guys only want one thing: sex. We also want food." Men absolutely want, love and need sex, but they also want, love, and need other things. Imagine how freeing it would be for Serita if her confidence was not based on her bedroom performance—if she could approach the first five-minute conversation, two-hour dinner, or half-day outing with a man feeling confident *she* was enough, that a man could be head-over-heels in love with her before they slept together. I wholeheartedly believe waiting to have sex after getting married strengthens the bond and the veneration you have for your partner and vice-versa. Studies have shown the benefits of waiting until marriage to have sex.

> The study was based on 2,035 married individuals who participated in an online assessment, which included questions such as, "When did you become sexual in this relationship?" A statistical analysis of participants showed that couples who wait until they put a ring on it enjoy significantly more benefits than those who had sex earlier: relationship stability was rated 22 percent higher; relationship satisfaction was rated 20 percent higher; sexual quality of the relationship was rated 15 percent better and communication was rated 12 percent better.

> "There's more to a relationship than sex, but we did find that those who waited longer were happier with the sexual aspect of their relationship," lead study author Dean Busby, a professor in Brigham Young University's School of Family Life, said in a release.

Why does waiting produce these benefits?

MY FRUIT IS MAGICAL

"I think it's because they've learned to talk and have the skills to work with issues that come up," Prof. Busby said.[8]

Sex is powerful and automatically changes the dynamic of any relationship. It has a way of attracting a considerable amount of focus in our lives and relationships. Unfortunately, thinking that sex will transform an unstable, unhealthy, or a casual relationship into a stable, healthy, or exclusive one is troubling and unrealistic.

As you might have guessed, 92 percent of men surveyed for my workshop research said sex was vital to a relationship. Some men said they enjoyed sex more given certain positive conditions, such as emotional and mental connection and feeling trust. One of the men I did a video interview with for the Silk Oyster, the pilot project of Love'n You, said, "great sex cannot save a bad relationship." This revelation came after a breakup with a live-in girlfriend.

What Serita and other women who rely too heavily on their sexual organs fail to realize is that these parts are limited in how much you can develop them to perform. In *The Outliers* by Malcom Gladwell, we see instances of people who learned and mastered a skill simply by working at it endlessly. He writes that we can master any skill we dedicate 10,000 hours of focused practice to. But there are some caveats. You can train your mind, spirit, and soul to accomplish the most amazing feats known to man. A person in their sixties can decide to commit and study to become an engineer. They can retrain their mind to grasp and master concepts that were once completely foreign to them. An agnostic can experience a spiritual awakening after years of belief that nothing is or can be known of

---

8   Dave McGinn, "Couples who wait report better sex lives," *The Globe and Mail*, December 22, 2010.

God. They can choose to explore their new found spirituality, and many do! But you cannot change the fiber or nature of your fruit. There are very real, widely experienced, and accepted limitations to the abilities of our physical being. You can develop your character, but your fruit will remain the same. Well, not quite. It can change, but eight out of ten times it does not get sexier. Age, childbirth and other factors might cause changes to your fruit that I will leave to your gynecologist to explain. I welcome you to use the most exotic blends of lavender and juniper berries to enhance its fragrance. Engage its muscles in daily Kegel exercises. Even go as far as the now trendy vaginal rejuvenation surgeries—which are really just creams and injections that should be taken with EXTREME caution and after consulting with a reputable gynecologist. But even if you only allow the finest silks from China near it, it still will not have magical powers. Sorry.

> An elderly couple was listening to a religious revival on the radio. The preacher ended his stirring speech by saying, "God wants to heal you all. Just stand up, put one hand on the radio, then place the other on the part of the body that is sick." The old woman tottered to her feet, put one hand on the radio and the other on her arthritic leg. The old man put one hand on the radio and one hand on his genitals. The old woman snapped at him, "Fred! This preacher said God would heal the sick, not raise the dead!"[9]

Sex plays a vital role in the enjoyment and strengthening of a marriage. It can help soothe partners after a tense and heated disagreement.

---

9   Billoo, Badhshah, *The Unofficial Joke Book of Smart Couples* (New Delhi: Fusion Books, 2004).

MY FRUIT IS MAGICAL

Sex can help punctuate an achievement or joyous occasion or it can just be a random pastime. But irrespective of why we come together to engage in it, sex is an enjoyable experience that enhances already strong and healthy relationships. But relying too heavily on your sexual ability to sustain a marriage would be like serving someone dessert after every meal: yes, it is delicious and at times intoxicating, but if that is all there is, it feels empty and will eventually be undesirable. If that dessert is accompanied by a substantial, nourishing meal that leaves just enough room for more, then it becomes the perfect icing on the cake, so to speak. The presence of other elements enhances the enjoyment of the dessert over time. In the same way, it is important to appeal to all of a man's desires, not just his sexual ones.

Earlier I went through a list of rhetorical questions I would have liked to ask Serita about the value she placed on her fruit: Would it provide a warmth comforting enough to make him forget he had just lost his job? Would it be strong enough to hold the home together after he had lost his mom and spiraled into depression? Is it so fragile that he would devote every waking thought to how to protect and cherish it? Would it remain exotic and sensual enough to make his client who looks like a supermodel seem like chopped liver to him? Is her fruit magical?

I am almost certain the answers to these questions would be "No." But I concede if she engaged her significant other on multiple levels—emotionally, spiritually, socially, and intellectually—he may actually attribute her fruit with supernatural abilities it does not actually possess. Because he is fulfilled all around in the relationship (to the extent that it is mutual) it naturally strengthens their bond. And each time he recalls or engages in sex with her it will be in the context of that bond. In this full, well rounded, whole relationship, her fruit might actually seem magical.

LILY B. DONKOR

Biblical Insight

My fruit is magical

The cover of this book is an obvious ode to the account of Adam and Eve in the Bible. It is no secret by now that my approach and beliefs are Biblically based. I am inspired daily by the stories, characters, lessons, struggles and overall theme of this timeless book. But when considering the lie *My Fruit Is Magical,* not even one or two distinct verses came to mind. I could not recall or even find a Bible verse that explicitly addressed the vagina as not having enchanting powers. Does this actually mean my notion is not found or grounded in the Bible? Certainly not.

We have a *no screens on school nights* rule at our home. That means our seven-year-old son and three-year-old daughter are not allowed to be on any devices from Sunday evening until Friday after school. They are free to play with toys, do activities, do homework, read or clean the house (that last one is wishful thinking). It is important to know our firstborn, David II is a rule follower (as firstborn children generally are). His father and I are always very impressed with how mature and considerate he is—and we let him know it. But during the first week of being in the second grade, he was sitting at the dining room table, boldly scrolling through my iPad. Is this a joke? How could he be so brazen and not even try to hide this obvious disobedience?

"David, did we not tell you and Dior there is no screen time from Sunday to Thursday?

Without looking up at me he said "Yes, but the rest of my homework is on my class reading app. I should be done in about thirty minutes".

"Oh, ok". I said, walking away impressed but a little embarrassed.

My son understood the implied meaning of the *no screen rule.* The

MY FRUIT IS MAGICAL

point of the rule was to eliminate mindless screen watching and video games. They were free to engage in anything else including toys that stimulate their creativity, imagination and challenge their comprehension. And doing his homework on a screen certainly fits into what they were allowed to do. In the same way, although the Bible does not explicitly say the vagina is not magical, the implied meaning is there.

In the narrative of Samson and Delilah, Delilah was able to get Samson to do her bidding and most people think it is because she seduced him sexually. And if you were to take a poll of what comes to mind about Samson and Delilah, a great number of people would mention sex. The fact is, the Bible never mentioned that the two had sex at all. A similar narrative occurred in the New Testament between Herod and Salome. She simply danced for him and later convinced him to behead John the Baptist. In both cases, Salome and Delilah's fruits were not the tools used in getting their way (I will unpack the problematic natures of both sets of relationships as ones not to envy or emulate in a subsequent blog or book). Both women achieved their goals (albeit sinister) without the use of their fruits.

The story of Rachel and Leah in Genesis 29 & 30 can be outright comical if it was not so disturbing. These two sisters end up married to the same man and spend years trying to win his loyalty and affection with sex and child bearing. They both gave their female assistants to Jacob as well, hoping to score points for their respective teams. But the madness does not stop there. They even traded actual fruit (mandrakes) for the prize of sleeping with Jacob, their husband, for one night. Both Rachel and Leah were heavily vested in doing anything humanly possible to make him prefer her over the other. Neither they, nor their assistants were mentioned as being more remarkable than the other. Their fruits were not magical.

If you think Jacob had more sexual partners than he could handle, then

Solomon did the impossible. One thousand wives and concubines. If he had sex with only one of his women a day it would take almost three years to revisit the first woman. Yet, none were so outstandingly remarkable to keep him exclusively for herself. Solomon did not find five magical fruits out of one thousand! In Ecclesiastes Chapter 2, Solomon takes a survey of his life and the many pleasures he has had. He mentions his real estate, his livestock, servants, money, his children, the knowledge he acquired, but there is no mention of his sexual exploits. I am sure by now you can grasp the implied meaning the way my seven-year-old did. Just because something is not named does not mean we cannot glean a valuable lesson from a stated general principle.

The Bible puts a strong emphasis on wisdom and wise counsel in building our lives and relationships, not sex. In fact, there are over two hundred accounts of the word wisdom throughout the text. As we close out this chapter, I want you to understand what sets you apart are your character, insights, work ethic, and other intangible qualities that can be improved upon. As you consider the next few years of your life as a single or married woman, desire and go after wisdom. Let your house be built on a sturdy foundation. Proverbs 14:1 (AMP) says, "The wise woman builds her house [on a foundation of godly precepts, and her household thrives],

But the foolish one [who lacks spiritual insight] tears it down with her own hands [by ignoring godly principles]."

Lasting Love Notes:

1. Great sex becomes far more meaningful with a partner who stimulates other (emotional, mental, spiritual, social, etc.) desires.

MY FRUIT IS MAGICAL

2. Over time, allow a man to enjoy and discover all the intrinsic traits and values you have before he ever has a chance to earn discovering the most intimate part of you.

3. Great sex alone is not sufficient to sustain a lasting, meaningful relationship.

Please do not ascribe mystic qualities to what has been scientifically proven to be the same across cultures, ethnic groups, and nations. Your fruit is unique and special (to the extent that it is attached to a unique and special you), and can spice up an already enjoyable relationship, but in and of itself, it is not magical.

CHAPTER 6
We Don't Need to Label It to Make It Real

Most of us can agree that dating is more of a free-form dance than a sport. There are not really any fixed rules. We all dance to the beat of our own drums or completely ignore the tempo but still have a great time doing it. Music and dancing give us permission to let loose and allow things to just happen as they will. No real rules restrict us or dictate how much the pulse of our heartbeats should match the sway of our hips. We just go for it! Most of us are born into structured circumstances, and we leave the earth the same way. When we leave the solitary walls of the womb, we are greeted by a team of professionals operating under the strictest of medical guidelines. Our parents are advised to put babies on a schedule. From daycare to high school, we are expected to be in class, and whether we pass is determined in part by our attendance records. Boundaries tell us what is acceptable but also define what is not. It lets others know our expectations of them and us, theirs. When terms are not clearly stated or understood, chaos and mishandled feelings tend to follow.

During my undergraduate years, I had a part-time job at a telecommunications company which paid about fifty percent of my bills. The other half of my income was made through various side hustles like doing hair, babysitting, and occasionally, being a server at private functions. I got started with serving through my God-mother and financial mentor. She is a highly successful and sought-after financial advisor and business owner. I believe God placed her in my life at the exact time He knew I needed immense guidance, support, and structure. She lovingly mentored me and kept me accountable for my decisions. She never let me feel sorry for myself or wallow in self-pity. I strongly advise getting mentors: Mentors who will hold you accountable and honest. She knew I was struggling financially to meet my obligations and rather than giving me money, she pointed out opportunities for me to earn money. She introduced me to a caterer friend of hers that needed servers at the many events for which she provided catering services. The events were often on Friday and Saturday nights and I would begin setting up at about 6:00 p.m., serve for the duration of the event and clean up for another hour or two after the function. It was tiring work but it was paid work. A friend of mine insisted on accompanying me to one of these gigs after I shared some humorous incidents I witnessed while serving. I asked my boss and she did not object to me bringing company. My friend, we will call her Tanya, did virtually every task I did. She served, cleaned, ran errands, washed dishes, you name it. It was fantastic! The night went by much faster, more enjoyably and far less tiring than other nights. At the end of the shift, my boss paid me our agreed upon amount, we said our goodbyes and Tanya and I left. The next time I had a similar gig (at this point I had partnered up with a few different caterers), Tanya insisted on coming with me again. I found it odd that she was working for free but she seemed to really enjoy herself and she never once mentioned compensation. She accompanied me to almost a dozen catering events before she suddenly stopped. As usual, I called her a few days before a gig to tell her when and where I would be working and asked if she wanted to join me. There was dead silence on the phone for a few seconds. Then came the explosion. Tanya was upset with me and accused me of being a selfish friend. She insisted I should have appealed to my bosses on her behalf to contract with her or at least pay her for the occasions she worked. I rebutted that she did not even make it known to me that she wanted employment. 'You said you wanted to come and you enjoyed the experience. You did not mention anything about getting paid'. She did not take too kindly to that response.

This reminds me of a type of relationship that seems to be in vogue lately, where the terms are not spelled out and both parties seem to be okay with it on the surface. These relationships can begin in any number of ways. Sometimes they are a result of two strangers "hooking up" after knowing each other for a matter of hours, or sometimes friends suddenly develop romantic feelings for one another and explore those feelings. Either way, the two never really verbalize the expectation of an exclusive relationship, or formally confer the title of boyfriend or girlfriend. The relationship remains undefined for months and sometimes years. Whether such relationships are a fad or here to stay, I am not sure. I cannot fully wrap my mind around the idea of a casual relationship without a formal commitment, but it is understood that emotional, sexual, and at times financial gratification is all part of the package. I understand there is a slew of adult relationships that are transactional or sordid in nature, but that is not what is confusing here. The reason these informal "let's not put a label on it" relationships are so baffling is because too often females who insist they are "just talking," or "just want to see where things end up," end up being surprised, upset, and confused that their lover is now engaged to someone he has known for less than a year.

I have sat with plenty of jilted females after one of these episodes. They all recite the litany of reasons men gave them about why it was not time to make it official. They would then belabor the point that the man was not the settling-down type, and his new girl would be sorry when he left her. Yet a few months prior, their relationship was fluid and was not to be labeled. There were no expectations. He had never officially recognized her as his exclusive girlfriend, and she had never insisted he make their relationship official. They enjoyed each other's company and satisfied one another's needs for the time they were "together." If she had persisted in defining their relationship, she might have been the one getting married to him, or at the very least understanding he had no plans on marrying her.

I understand that not all women are the same, and some may very well be capable of moving on without so much as a thought; however, the vast number of women I have encountered, counselled, coached or read about are not wired that way. Their emotions do get invested in these unlabeled and casual relationships. I have found that some ladies enter into these sorts of arrangements because they have come to believe guys prefer them. They think men prefer women who demand nothing of them, are willing to accommodate their desires and are not "emotional" like other girls. Hence, they conclude that men will like you more if you put out and then get out, only to find the same man began a devoted relationship after you parted ways. This sort of relationship uncertainty does not benefit you in the short or long term. We are wired to anticipate and prepare for what lies ahead of us; to plan and look toward desired outcomes. It gives a sense of certainty and control when I budget my income based on the assurance of a steady paycheck. The reason I can count on that income as an employee is because my employer and I have agreed on the terms of our working relationship and as long as those terms are in place, there is a sense of security. Of course, circumstances can alter or dissolve our agreement, but in most professional working arrangements, there are built in safeguards to mitigate excess loss. Simply put, the sense of permanence that a committed relationship offers is far better for your overall mental health than an undefined working or romantic relationship."

"Marriage is often accompanied by a sense of relationship permanence, and despite the relatively high rate of divorce in the United States, marriages are much more likely to last than other relationships like cohabitations (Brines and Joyner 1999).[10] Since relationship dissolution may harm mental health, relationship stability may explain positive effects of marriage on mental health. For example, Brown (2000)[11] attributes the heightened depression of cohabitors (vis-à-vis married individuals) to their relationship instability."[12]

---

10 Julie Brines and Kara Joyner, *The Ties That Bind: Principles of Cohesion in Cohabitation and Marriage* (American Sociological Review. 1999;64:333–355.).

11 Susan L. Brown, *The Effect of Union Type on Psychological Well-Being: Depression among Cohabitors Versus Marrieds* (Journal of Health and Social Behavior. 2000;41:241–255.).

12 Jeremy E. Uecker J Health Soc Behav. 2012 Mar; 53(1): 67–83. Published online 2012 Feb 9. doi: 10.1177/0022146511419206

LILY B. DONKOR

Knowing, defining, and then communicating your desire for a committed relationship is one of the best moves you can make for yourself and your partner. I want you to take note of Cordelia's experience with this myth.

A Coupling Narrative

Cordelia and Sam met in the lobby of his apartment; he was collecting his mail and she was exiting the building after a study session with classmates. Cordelia is twenty-six and working on her master's degree in chemistry. She has a part-time job at a cosmetics lab downtown and occasionally socializes with colleagues after work at the local bistro.

Sam is twenty-five and moved into the apartment complex seventeen months ago after starting his career at a marketing firm he and his business partner began three years earlier. His business partner is Bright, a forty-five-year-old navy veteran who decided to go back to college. He and Sam met in their microeconomics class in college and hit it off. They and three others were assigned a group project to come up with a campaign for a supply chain firm trying to expand into Africa. They did so well on that project that Sam revamped the campaign and pitched it to a few companies. He decided to include Bright because he valued his experience and work ethic. The two have since pitched a series of campaigns and landed a few deals in the process.

Cordelia and Sam were both interested in one another

at first sight, but neither acknowledged the other. They had a second-chance encounter a few weeks later in the elevator, and this time neither was willing to let the opportunity slip away. "HI!" they both said a bit too eagerly. They spent the next hour chatting outside the front doors of the apartment building. After that day, they spent any free time they had together—which was not much since they were both very busy people.

They passionately enjoyed each other's company but resolved not to text during the day and to keep the phone calls to a minimum when they were busy with work or school. As much as Cordelia liked Sam, she did not want to be the one to ruin a good thing by labeling it. She would often ignore him for a few days or weeks at a time to distance herself from him—it was her coping mechanism to avoid getting hurt or disappointed. Sam really liked her, but he figured she was not as invested in a relationship as he was since she would disappear and not think it necessary to tell him why.

On a Friday afternoon, Bright stopped by Sam's to pick up a package and met Cordelia for the first time.

"Hey, Bright, this is Cordelia, my..."

Before Sam could get the words out, Cordelia anxiously said, "I'm Cordelia, Sam's friend. Nice to meet you."

When Bright left, Cordelia, wanting to ease the tension, told Sam not to dwell on her use of the word "friend" because "we are just seeing where things end up." And that was the end of their exclusive relationship as far as Sam was concerned. She, on the other hand, felt better about their relationship and thought, "Now he knows I am willing to take things at his pace." Sam told

Bright he was ready to settle down, and since Cordelia was not, he was open to finding someone who was. But he and Cordelia continued to hang out and hook up.

Cordelia graduated the following month and got a full-time job offer with great benefits as a formulator chemist at the cosmetics lab. She invited the two boys for drinks to celebrate her good news when Sam introduced some good news of his own. He brought along his new girlfriend and introduced her to his friends Bright and Cordelia.

Know your intentions for entering a relationship—any relationship. If you change your mind, be sure to communicate that to ensure both of you are on the same page. If you are, great! If you're not, you now have an opportunity to talk about it. Find out if you both want to continue, and discuss your relationship goals. It is often said, jokingly, that women expect men to read their minds. Do away with the guesswork or the joke might be on you.

C. Morgan wrote, "Setting boundaries is a way of caring for myself. It doesn't make me mean, selfish, or uncaring because I don't do things your way. I care about me too." Being in a relationship can be emotionally taxing in itself; why compound the levels of uncertainty? The least you owe yourself is knowing what his intentions are. If he wants to marry you, great; if not, that is fine too. If he wants marriage but he is not sure with whom, even better. At least you will know how to proceed, and that you have some things to clarify with him, but more importantly with yourself. An undefined relationship keeps you in a constant state of anxiety. Define your relationship so you can truly move forward with confidence.

My dear friend, understand what you will and will not accept before you enter a relationship. This does not mean that you demand he refers to you as his girlfriend within a week of meeting. But it does mean if you have any doubt about your role in his life, it is probably an appropriate time to have a heart-to-heart conversation about your relationship. I want you to know that you are precious, and if he is the right one for you, he will recognize that as well. At a stage in the relationship when you feel you have both invested a lot of yourselves, verbalize how you define your relationship over dinner or a nice relaxing stroll.

The reason you are with him and he is with you is because you are interested in one another at some level. You should never feel you are putting a burden on your relationship by setting goals and expectations. Rather, defining these things will provide clarity and the freedom to enjoy one another with trust and openness.

Biblical Insight

Most Christians are no stranger to Habakkuk 2:2. It has been sermonized for various topics: from setting a standard for one's family; to understanding the codes of conduct that govern nations.

The Common Jewish Bible translation frames it like this:

"Write down the vision clearly on tablets, so that even a runner can read it."

Understanding the why of any endeavor will make the difference between being busy and being productive. A romantic relationship, at the very least, is certainly a time and emotionally demanding endeavor. But before you can even ask why you are in the relationship; I think it is wise to be certain you are in a relationship. I have counselled and consoled too many who believed they were in a mutually exclusive relationship but were confused, hurt and angry when they learnt otherwise. They performed all the same roles boyfriends and girlfriends do. They spent extended amounts of time together; they spent money on each other or shared a bank account, they were physically and emotionally intimate; in some cases, friends and family of their "partner" welcomed them with open arms. In the end, the many romantic relationship indicators did not automatically equal a romantic relationship.

"Write down the vision clearly on tablets, so that even a runner can read it." As I have mentioned before, your time and resources are precious and should be guarded. What those words spoken by God in Habakkuk 2:2 does for me is prompt me to look at what goals my family and I are working toward and see if I am on task. It helps me to delay or deny what does not promote our overall vision. Having our clear vision in mind guides my decisions. I know whether to spend more or less time and resources on a person, a place or a purchase. It helps to justify everyday decisions I am unsure of. Although you may be running a hundred miles an hour getting work done, spending time with family, eating right and working out, couponing, grooming and raising kids, cooking, closing deals, decluttering, changing your wardrobe, spending time with friends, and so forth—are you still on task? There should be such clarity about your relationship status that even while running a hundred miles an hour through life, you know where you stand. If you are not confident or clear at any point about your arrangement, it is time to ask some questions. This is not to say you need to demand a status your partner is not ready for. It is so you are not blindsided. It is so you can keep running at your desired pace without trying to decipher mixed or unclear signals.

Lasting Love Notes:

1. Know your reasons for entering into a relationship—and communicate it clearly.

2. Do not fall into the trap of downplaying your desire for a committed relationship for fear of losing him.

3. Avoid romantic relationships that demand from you in the short term, but have no long-term potential.

If you think not labelling your relationship increases the chances of its success, think again. Defining and setting goals with your partner about your relationship ensures better odds of a lasting union than just "seeing where things end up."

CHAPTER 7
Two Can Play That Game

Many things in life are based on unwritten, yet widely understood and accepted rules. For example, you cannot go around hitting others; keep your hands to yourself. Do not give birth and abandon your young; babies need the care of a parent or guardian. Another rule concerns female monogamy versus male polygamy: if you are a woman, do not sleep around. Compared to past centuries, men are now more likely to couple with or marry a woman who is not a virgin; there is no argument there. However, men are far less accepting of women who have had numerous sexual partners than women are of men who have had multiple partners. Irrespective of race, nationality, or ethnicity, the overwhelming consensus is that men still prefer a "good girl" to settle down with. Yes, we as a society are more liberal now than we were half a century ago, but if you are banking on finding more men who could not care less that you have been sexually overactive,

LILY B. DONKOR

you might need to wait for another half century. Let us look at the case of Esosa and Brendon.

A Coupling Narrative

Esosa and Brendon were childhood friends. She can still recall the day she and her family, the Lawals, moved into the brown brick house next to Brendon's home. He lived with his parents and two cousins, who were at least five years older than he was and could not keep their eyes off Esosa's mother, Ade. Esosa could not really blame them. Everyone thought her mom was out-of-this-world gorgeous—and Esosa agreed. She was five foot seven with a twenty-four-inch waist, thirty-two-inch hips, and sculpted cheekbones that seemed to gently cradle her sultry, soft brown eyes. While Esosa lacked her mother's physique, she made up for this with her smile. Her dad always teased her by saying that when he met Ade, he knew her rapturous smile would leave him half broke, but when Esosa was born, he knew her smile would completely wipe him out.

When the family was moving in, Brendon's cousins abandoned their books and magazines on the porch to welcome the Lawals to the neighborhood and began helping them move their belongings into the newly remodeled house. Brendon was twelve at this time and did not even look up from his Game Boy system. It was not until two years later when Esosa turned thirteen that Brendon asked her to be his girlfriend.

Brendon's family knew of and accepted their relationship. Esosa would spend time at Brendon's house in his absence, hanging out with his mom and aunts in the kitchen or on the porch. They would take turns styling her thick light brown hair, which she often wore in a high bun accented with three two-strand twists above her left temple.

But Esosa did not dare tell her parents she was dating, although her younger brother was aware but could not have cared less. The Lawals had zero tolerance for kids dating before college. They would often say, "It's a senseless distraction that is crippling the Western world." As long as Esosa and her brother stayed focused and maintained a minimum A average, there would be peace at home. And for the sake of peace Esosa was content to leave the fact that she had been with Brendon for three years now at her front steps.

She knew that Brendon had many cousins who visited frequently, but lately a handful of new female "cousins" were visiting the house late in the evenings, at hours when Ade insisted, "Only criminals and lowlifes with no ambition stay out at odd hours of the night." Brendon assured Esosa they really were his cousins and even introduced one of them to her as such. His family knew he was sleeping with a few of them, and when Esosa finally confronted him, his aunts tried to pacify her with, "He loves you—they are just for fun."

She felt embarrassed and enraged. How could women who seemed to love her as their own daughter—they had braided her hair, taught her to cook Brendon's favorite food, and attended her violin performance for the mayor—hurt her so deeply? How was cheating, and at such a rate and with multiple "side chicks," okay with anyone, especially his "mothers"?

Esosa was not going to be anybody's victim! It was time to level the playing field. She dated frequently and made a point of having her dates drop her in her neighborhood—close enough for Brendon and his pitiful family and friends to notice but far enough that her mom and dad were unaware. Although she was a freshman in college and was allowed to date, she had no intention of introducing any of these guys to her parents.

The irony was, she really did not enjoy dating that much—nor was she actually sleeping with different guys. She did, however, strongly believe that if a woman wanted to have multiple boyfriends simultaneously and have sex with a few, it was perfectly fine. She knew the rumors swirling around about her and did not bother to dissuade anyone who thought she was promiscuous. As far as she was concerned, it was high time they all stepped into the twenty-first century!

Whether she wanted this news to spread beyond Brendon's immediate circle was now no longer relevant. By the time she completed her sophomore year in college, her acquaintances got wind of her so-called boyfriends and weekend trips in different cars. She still did not care.

In her final year, Esosa went on to meet a serious boyfriend, Scott. She was over the moon with excitement as she wrapped up a phone call with him the night before her graduation. She would be graduating *summa cum laude* (with the highest distinction) from her engineering program. She had made her parents proud and the new 2010 Acura TL in the driveway was proof!

That summer she continued her paid internship at the football stadium, where she bumped into Scott. She had not spoken to him for almost a week but chalked it up to adjusting to her new schedule. He had actually been avoiding her. Scott met some of Esosa and Brendon's friends and family during graduation for the first time and had since become very friendly with Brendon's oldest cousin.

Scott did not have the courtesy to explain to her why "he no longer had time for a serious relationship," but once she noticed his car frequenting her cul-de-sac to visit Brendon's cousin and the family, she knew why. That he would be so simple-minded to believe the lies of people he barely knew without asking her what was going on repulsed her. How could she have not seen his naïveté during the seven months they were together? What kind of ignorant man makes such a callous decision without taking all the evidence, or lack of it, into account? Scott, that's who. Her Scotty... the one she still loved.

There are varying opinions on monogamy and the double standard that exists around the subject of dating. I will tell you the same thing I often tell my mentees: we all have to live with the choices we have made, and the consequences of those choices. If your potential spouse asks if you have any debt, be prepared to answer even if it is not going to be a comfortable discussion. If the question is about previous sexual partners (which some marriage counselors advise against asking about), be prepared to answer that as well. It is always a good rule of thumb to make decisions, especially in adulthood, that you are willing to stand behind.

> A guy is reading his paper when his wife walks up behind him and smacks him on the back of the head with a frying

> pan. He asks, "What was that for?" She says, "I found a piece of paper in your pocket with Betty Sue written on it." He says, "Jeez, honey, remember last week when I went to the track? Betty Sue was the name of the horse I went there to bet on." She shrugs and walks away. Three days later he is reading his paper when she walks up behind him and smacks him on the back of the head again with the frying pan. He asks, "What was that for?" She answers, "Your horse called."[13]

Make your decisions based on your core values. Period. If you feel a need to cheat or one-up the other person, you have probably veered off your desired path. Be true to yourself! Be confident, and do not let anyone get a rise or other negative reaction out of you.

It has been said that "Promiscuity is like never reading past the first page. Monogamy is like reading the same book over and over again."[14] If you are like me and look forward to enjoying the twists and turns of the entire book, getting to know the characters deeply, and indulging in the accomplishment of having finished what you started, good for you.

As I mentioned in the introduction of this book, I acknowledged and understood my advantages as a girl. I use them along with the skills I have developed to shape the reality I want. With anything in life, it is up to you to discover what *your* strengths, assets, and viewpoints are. Do not be afraid or ashamed to build a life you would be proud of with those tools and skills. Never feel cornered enough to act out of character simply to get

---

13 Joy Online, "Just for Laughs, Dec. 12, 2014. http://myjoyonline.com/news/just-for-laughs

14 Mason Cooley (1927 – Jul. 25, 2002). American Aphorist.

even. Ask yourself why you are choosing to explore your sexuality with multiple partners. Is this a reaction to a past experience? Was your aim to find love but sex happened instead? Knowing what you know now, would you have gone down the same path? I hope your answers to these questions guide you to make wise decisions that will pass the test of time, circumstance, and love.

Biblical Insight

Two can play that game

Do not say, "I will do to him just as he has done to me; I will pay him back according to what he has done."

PROV 24:29 (NET)

As you have probably figured out by now, I frequent the book of proverbs. There are boundless insights to be found in this book. There is not a situation I have gotten into that this good book has not been able to offer direction, correction, or a complete solution. I do not know about you but if I knew someone who always had the answer to any problem, I would make that person a part of my life in one form or another. I can truthfully and confidently say, the Bible has been great to me!

In the period I lived in Norway, I was fortunate enough to counsel countless individuals and couples—I either met them at church, panels, and workshops I was speaking at, or at social events. The sessions spanned the spectrum from as informal as a thirty-minute phone call, to an hour in the office with a box of tissues and a notepad. And as stated in the introduction, my method of helping anyone is typically informed by my examined life experience and proven wisdom from the Bible.

I will always remember a couple my husband and I counselled during this season. I have never met a more comedic and livelier couple. They were both such fun people to have around and their unique sense of humor was an experience to be applauded. They could narrate an incident that happened as mundane as brushing teeth and turn it into a twenty-minute bit of punch lines with the other spouse ad-libbing flawlessly.

As I got to know this couple more intimately, I quickly learnt their compatible sense of humor was matched only by their equally compatible sense of retribution. On one occasion the husband was upset with his wife and he decided to punish her by withholding money she needed for a specific time sensitive task. She got back at him by hiding his eyeglasses—and he is legally blind without them!

"Do not say, 'I will do to him just as he has done to me; I will pay him back according to what he has done.'" How can a person find peace of mind, a sense of security or happiness in such a combative environment? I can assure you this sort of behavior did not begin after they got married. The need to resort to such tactics reveals a deep-seated sense of insecurity. But the irony is, the more this couple one-upped each other, the more insecure they became because they were never sure when the other would sabotage or deliberately hurt them in some way.

Imagine if one of them decided enough was enough. If the husband made up his mind to no longer retaliate his wife's aggression. Instead, he would take the time to find out what is behind the malicious actions. Imagine he did that for three months. How about six months? A year? I have no doubt she would have put down her weapon. If you find yourself often looking for ways to respond to a hurtful act by your partner with a hurtful act of your own, it is time to think twice. In fact, do not even think twice. Simply follow the directives of Proverbs 24:29. Leave mind games out of your relationship. There are countless situations that call for us to be tactical, on guard and defensive; your romantic relationship is NOT one of them.

Lasting Love Notes:

1. Make decisions you are willing and ready to stand behind in relationships.

2. Be true to yourself. Let your course through love and relationships be guided by your principles and morals—not passing trends or a desire to get even.

3. Your heart is precious, so avoid games, tactics, and tricks in relationships.

You're only hurting yourself when you act out of character in destructive ways. "Anger, resentment, and jealousy doesn't change the heart of others—it only changes yours." I hope you never lose sight of what is important to you in an attempt to get even or prove a point. Stay true to yourself, and the rest will take care of itself.

CHAPTER 8
A Relationship Is Supposed to Make Me Happy

I absolutely love joyful people. They remind me of those enormous balloons in the shape of cartoon characters that you see in front of car dealerships—the ones that flail around all over the place. Have you ever been driving and barely noticed one because it was lying almost flat on the ground? The amazing thing about them is, before you can bat an eye, they rise again until they bounce into an upright stance with the most animated expressions on their faces. This is what comes to mind every time I see a truly joyful person. Naturally, the woes or adverse circumstances of life may knock them down, but they do not typically stay knocked down. Because the joy they have is not necessarily from their circumstances and surroundings—the external world. With a bit of time and intentionality, they regain their joy. They bounce back to being themselves again.

The kind of happiness that comes from being content with yourself is not exclusive to the rich, tall, educated, or married among us. It can be found in people of all kinds.

And just as easy as it is to spot a happy person, the telltale signs of an unhappy person are easy to see. One of the dead giveaways of a morose individual is complaining. I always say complainers make me itch!

I had a colleague years ago at a tech firm we worked at—we will call her Neena—who could turn any interaction into an opportunity to complain or find cause to create rumors where there was none. She would have won the top prize at the Passive-Aggressive State Fair if there had been one. At work, when an internal email went out stating the company was pleased to announce Blue Jeans Friday, she said, "Isn't that nice for those who look good in blue? I prefer gray with stripes." I recall one instance where four of us were planning one of our annual employee engagement and appreciation events. We had to work with a particular theme in mind as we selected the venue, decor, food, prizes, games, and other components of a four-month-long engagement leading to the final event. At one meeting we spent an hour brainstorming and bouncing ideas off one another. At the end of the meeting, we had settled on two potential locations to host the final event. The following day, Neena sent me a message griping that Adam (who was not on the planning committee) had suggested we go to TopGolf, which was not one of the locations we were initially considering. She ranted about how terrible that idea was, and said that just because he wanted to play childlike games did not mean the rest of the office staff would want to. At a follow-up meeting a few days later, one of the other two collaborators suggested we have TopGolf host the party. They said Adam had suggested it to them and they thought it would fit this year's theme and be very interactive and fun. The location was convenient, we would not need to splurge on decor, and games and food could be customized to our exact specifications. Would you believe, before anyone else could, Neena chimed in, "I thought that was an excellent idea as well. We should contact them immediately to secure the date!"

One character trait of unhappy people is their inconsistent behavior. Their emotions can flip at the drop of a hat. They are unstable. Because they are unhappy with themselves, it overwhelms every other emotion. The times of temporary glee are robbed by the ever-present sense of dissatisfaction. Abraham Lincoln said, "Folks are usually about as happy as they make their minds up to be," and I completely agree. In fact, that was the exact sentiment my father-in-love expressed to David and me at our wedding reception. He said, "Make up your mind to be happy. It does not matter what happens around you. Just make up your mind to be happy." I have found when I decide to have a positive outlook about a situation, even if the circumstances are not necessarily favorable, I begin to see the good in that situation. If you start your day saying, "I am going to have a good day today," your thinking will likely alter your actions—you will smile more and be friendly to others who will also return the gestures. This in turn will contribute to a good day.

Happy people are pleased with who and what they are despite their circumstances, and they are always striving to improve and progress. On the other hand, some people are generally unhappy single, remain unhappy even in marriage, get divorced, and are still visibly miserable.

If you set out to look for someone who will make you happy, what you are saying is you want someone to fill a certain void. Someone who will transform your current disposition and situation. You want someone who will operate in your life as a minstrel of sorts, always responsible for keeping you upbeat, cheery, and content. I am sure you are beginning to see the problem with this concept. If you believe a relationship is supposed to bring you happiness, the instant it does the opposite, your mind will tell you to run. You will think, 'This person is making me unhappy—it is not worth it.' If you are happy on your own, you will approach an unhappy situation in a relationship with the aim of making it peaceful and joyous again.

Belinda Luscombe, author of *Marriageology: The Art and Science Of Staying Together*, writes, "...happy spouses make life easier for their partners because their partners aren't stressed by the fact that their closest companion is always in a bad mood, and they're not exhausted by efforts to jolly them along or under constant pressure not to upset them."[15] Why not choose to be a happy person rather than hoping to find a supplier of happiness in marriage.

A Coupling Narrative

> I have known Doreen a little over fifteen years, and every time she enters a room you know she has arrived. She is not loud or obnoxious in any way, but she carries a force that makes you stop doing whatever occupies you at that moment and pay her some attention. I appreciate her ability to make even the most distant of acquaintances feel as if they have been friends with her forever. She has a way of drawing you in and making you feel as if she is completely in tune with you and has a genuine concern for your situation. Doreen is simply remarkable for these qualities. She loves people and people love her!

---

15 Belinda Luscombe, "Happy People Make Their Spouses Healthier," *TIME: TIME Guide to Happiness 2020*, https://time.com/collection/guide-to-happiness/4506490/happy-people-make-their-spouses-healthier/

For as long as I have known her, she has always had a boyfriend—some more noteworthy than others. The longest relationship lasted six years including a four-month break, while her shortest one was seventy-two hours. I must say, that three-day fling was actually significant. His name was Chen, and he was a music producer who had just turned thirty-one.

Doreen and I were then in our mid-twenties. We met for coffee on one of my short visits to Toronto and caught up on each other's lives: careers, family, love, challenges, hair and fashion, and high school memories. We continued our stroll down memory lane as we window-shopped at the mall. As life would have it, we ran into Chen, a boy we had frequently crossed paths with on the way home from high school—he had not made much of an impression at that time. There was nothing boyish about Chen now. It was obvious he lived a healthy, active lifestyle. He wore a well-tailored blazer that was hitting all the right notes and sported a rugged but sweet five o'clock shadow. His voice was masculine and warm, suffused with the confidence of a man who knew he had your attention. I decided to let Doreen and Chen speak in private; besides, I had spotted a pair of shoes I liked.

The next time Doreen and I spoke, she began the conversation with "I don't know what I was expecting out of this, but..." To make a long story short, Chen had gone out of town for work for two weeks, and they had decided to meet up when he returned. They spoke every day while he was away, and when he returned, he asked her to be his girlfriend. They cooked together, played board games, and attended her company party before going their separate ways.

Doreen has had a few decent boyfriends over the years, but she has yet to figure out why she has not found the one. But what she is certain of is the immense happiness she feels when she is with someone. The desire to get married is never too far from her consciousness, and she beams at the thought that the next relationship, the next man, could be the one. Looking over her life, she admits she is most fulfilled when she is in a relationship, and she wants that happy feeling to last longer. She figures marriage will be the magic elixir that will grant her this long-term happiness.

One thing I have noticed during the many phone sessions with Doreen is how she has idealized marriage. She has romanticized it to the point that she envisions what her husband should be like, how he should treat her, and how happy they will both be once they "become" one. I initially did not have the heart to tell her the reason Nolan—one of her longer-term boyfriends—changed his number was because she would subtly refer to other couples and attempt to diagnose why she thought they were happy. Her end goal was always that she and Nolan would reap the benefits of the lessons learned.

I have since explained to my unwitting friend that her pursuit of happiness is, in fact, a pursuit of clichés: boy meets girl; girl plays hard to get; boy plays along and gets girl after several planned alpha male gestures delivered with suave, gentlemanly chivalry that appears completely spontaneous; girl falls in love with boy, and every time girl feels insecure boy is always there to make her feel like a queen again. The reason Doreen is not finding happiness is that she thinks if everything works as it should, and he does what he ought to, then she will be happy. But in this new era of insatiable desires, when new is old by the time you hear about it, placing the burden of responsibility for your happiness on others—yes, even your own spouse—is a setup for a letdown.

I explained to Doreen that happiness can be cultivated between a couple once you are already happy with yourself. One reason her boyfriends leave or check out emotionally is because she projects her insecurities on them. She, like other single or unhappy ladies, looks for trouble where there is none. For example, imagine you were once perfectly happy with your planned dates every other weekend, but ever since Miss Jones started going on Tuesday dates with her man and you have noticed her always smiling in her Instagram pictures, you have developed a bad attitude while trying to enjoy eating your salad during your weekend dates. Seriously? I could write a book filled with the many petty comments I have heard friends, colleagues, and strangers make about their relationships compared to other people's. The trouble is that eight out of ten times the comparisons and complaints only make them bitter and not better. Benchmarking ourselves with others can be tremendously motivating but only if we have the mindset to improve. Keep in mind I said benchmarking *ourselves*, not our spouses. When it comes to others, it is no longer benchmarking—it is comparing.

Doreen has placed so high a premium on a fixed image of marriage and the notion of its built-in happiness that it has become almost impossible to convince her of life's realities. The reality that marriage is a constant state of compromise and collaboration—that to be happy in the long-term you will have many instances of denying yourself of your wants for the sake of mutually beneficial outcomes. The irony is that her obsession to be happy has driven away some chances of true happiness because she sabotages her relationships with unrealistic expectations.

I invite you now to go to lovenyou.org to spend a few minutes with *George & Naomi* to see how inner joy and the desire to make your partner happy can make your love journey immeasurably sweeter.

An example of my own shows the importance of not demanding too much of another person. I love being warm and find myself feeling cold more often than my husband. This used to result in our infamous Thermostat Wars. I would turn the thermostat up to between seventy-eight and eighty-one degrees, and he would turn it down to between seventy-two and seventy-four degrees. This would last for hours—up, down, up, down—until one of us fell asleep and the other won by default. As you can imagine this would get ridiculous, frustrating, and laughable all at the same time. One solution was to send ourselves to opposite sides of the house and be happy in our different climates. Another solution was to sit happily together on the couch—me with my laptop and blanket and him watching TV while the temperature remained at seventy-five degrees. My cold-toes dilemma was resolved under my cozy blanket, and I got to sit on the same couch and spend quality time (one of my love languages) with my dude. I could have insisted it was his responsibility to ensure I was comfortable and happy, but what would happen if he passed out from the unbearable heat?

Although your partner may not walk away from the relationship, he

MY FRUIT IS MAGICAL

might just check out emotionally, mentally, or even financially from your demands on him to make you happy. By constantly demanding he needs to do more to make you happy, you might be applying undue pressure on an otherwise acceptable relationship.

> A man goes to see a wizard and says, "Can you lift a curse that was put on me years ago?" "Maybe," says the wizard, "if you can remember the exact words of the curse." The man replies without hesitation, "I pronounce you man and wife..."[16]

When you make a personal commitment to be happy, you will be amazed by how much more enjoyable your relationship will be. Rather than seeing things from a negative or even "realistic" point of view, challenge yourself to see the positive. Take it upon yourself to cultivate an amiable atmosphere around you as much as it depends on you. You will find if you persevere in this manner, your positive attitude will begin to rub off on your partner.

Biblical Insight

A happy heart is good medicine and a joyful mind causes healing,
But a broken spirit dries up the bones.

PROV 17:22 (AMP)

When writing this chapter, the words of wisdom my father-in-love

---

[16] Jokes-Best, "Funny Family Jokes," retrieved 2008.

shared at our wedding reception kept coming to mind. He did not speak for exceptionally long but he reiterated in different ways that we must make up our minds to be happy. At the time, I must admit I was underwhelmed by his speech. I was thinking to myself, this man founded a vibrant renowned church in Toronto, has since started more than thirty others (at the time of this writing there are over a hundred All Nations Full Gospel Churches around the world), he is the founder and president of the first university to launch a satellite in West Africa, has two PHds and this is the best speech he could come up with? Where are the lofty words of encouragement or the peculiar secrets of marriage? "Decide to be happy". That was it?

Turns out, that was all I needed. That four-word sentence made the difference between the worst two years of my marriage and the best years I have been experiencing ever since. What dad said was only a part of the wisdom of Proverbs 17:22. Every relationship has challenges, romantic ones or otherwise. It is typically the times of challenge and disagreement that the negative emotions we feel towards the other person come to the surface and are magnified. Because in the earlier years I sought for David to bring me joy, the fact that he caused the pain to begin with, would prolong the healing process. But when I decided joy was going to be my default emotional state and I engaged in behavior, habits, and relationships that facilitated that, my marriage changed. So now when we disagree intensely or I am unhappy about a situation, my mind is able to bring about the healing as Proverbs 17:22 says. It is not just a matter of being happy, it is rather being joyful at my core—to the extent that I bring my own joy and happiness into every situation. My happiness has become a weapon to diffuse any gloom that threatens to cast a shadow on my marriage and other cherished relationships. When my default state was not one of happiness, even after the argument had ended, I would get angrier and sadder with time. Why was this? The last part of the Bible verse says, "But a broken spirit dries up the bones."

The Common Jewish Translation uses the word 'strength' instead of bones. Unhappiness or a broken spirit will sap the last bit of strength or happiness that the initial disappointment did not take. How miserable does that sound?! Yet, this is what often happens; people just do not recognize it.

I heard the words of my father-in-love during his speech but that did not change me. I had been reading my Bible for years and I would still get into the pit of unhappiness after a heated fight. So, what changed? I made up my mind to be happy. Period. I knew I did not have the power to will happiness or joy for myself and that is where this passage became a game changer for me. By meditating on this verse and many others about how God has the best plans for me and how truly blessed I am, I am constantly filling my heart with joy and the amazing truth of God's love for me. A disagreement about our car, or how to discipline the kids or respond to a crisis in ministry does not change the truth of God's word and its effect on my heart.

Friend, make up your mind to be happy! And for me, the Word of God is the best source to get refilled.

Lasting Love Notes:

1. Make up your mind to be happy. There is something very attractive about a person who is joyful and can face life's challenges with a smile.

2. Placing the burden of responsibility for your happiness on another person will only drain that relationship. Your partner may grow helpless in an attempt to keep you cheery, and you will be left in a state of constant disappointment.

3. Rather than looking for a relationship to make you happy, propose to make your relationship a happy and pleasant one.

A relationship cannot instantly alter your state of mind for the worse—nor can it instantly make you feel better. I have encountered some married women who are deliriously happy. I have also met some whose unhappiness is palpable. And for those at both extremes, the deciding variable is not money, social status, religion, or any one thing you can pinpoint. Having a positive and upbeat outlook on life has nothing to do with the situation you are in but everything to do with how you choose to see it. If you lack joy before marriage, you might be hard pressed to find it in marriage.

In a nutshell, relationships work best when two emotionally stable individuals come together to share in each other's happiness.

CONCLUSION
Your Love Story

The purpose of this book is to debunk eight lies we commonly hear about dating and maintaining love. My desire is for you to give yourself the best chance possible to write your own love story. I want you to begin your love journey from a place of strength and confidence and never from one of desperation or insecurity. I hope by interacting with the love story videos on *For Better*, you are now more excited about your prospects of finding and keeping love. Your love story does not begin when you find someone; it begins right now in the way you choose to see yourself and the value you will bring to a relationship. My wish is for you to rid your current and future relationships of these eight lies and pursue love with wisdom and an open heart.

I want you to ditch the myth that says you have to have fun , as if a dreary life awaits you in marriage. Go ahead and live a fulfilling life now, but know there is a lot more excitement awaiting you when you marry the right person. So, get out there, take risks, and meet new people; you just might run into Mr. Right.

And because first impressions matter, take ownership of the first impressions you make by looking your best and wearing a smile. Do not hold on to the hope that he will like you for what is on the inside first. As we now know, God was not chastising Samuel for not looking at David's heart to determine if he was king material. God was simply stating a fact. He was telling Samuel the reason he was not able to see David's potential is because he, Samuel, did not have the capability to see the contents of David's character, the heart, at first glance. A potential partner may in due course see how incredible you are, but at first glance, they can only see your smile, your hair, your clothes, your actions, and your reactions. What impression do you want to give in the first minute of meeting you?

As you are taking chances and building your social currency, keep your future in mind. Think about how your experiences can serve to make you more marketable and profitable in the coming years. Gone are the days where men were the sole breadwinners, so do not fall into the trap of thinking that he has to be able to provide for you. Instead, unlock your own potential to earn a living.

And as you climb that ladder to success, be open to the possibility of finding love along the way. Do not restrict yourself to the myth that you need to be established first. Allow yourself to consider the possibility that a man can come into your life when you least expect it! There is something thrilling about unexpectedly meeting someone who seems to just get you. Enjoy the chemistry and attraction between you while showcasing your many wonderful qualities that will keep a relationship thriving!

By now I'm certain you do not still believe—if you ever did—that your fruit is magical. And by the time you reach this conclusion and have enjoyed the accompanying love stories, I hope you will decide to be more purposeful and confident in the way you approach relationships.

I also hope you no longer think you do not need to label a relationship to make it real. Leave the guessing game alone. I know your time and love are precious to you, so be certain the efforts you are putting into a relationship are worthwhile. Be tactful and intentional about the questions you ask in determining if you are both on the same page about the direction the relationship is headed. That way you can make a smart decision about what happens next.

It is for that same reason you must not allow yourself to feel cornered into thinking that two can play *that* game. I can confidently say, if you find yourself at a juncture where you need to get even in a relationship, it is probably best to walk away. No matter the type of relationship you find yourself in, it is never okay to abandon who you are. Know that you are special and the right person will come along who will recognize and appreciate your uniqueness.

And finally, never lose sight of what makes you content by investing all your hopes in the myth that a relationship is supposed to make you happy. Your general level of happiness is a good indicator of how happy you will be in a relationship. Choose to be happy right now, where you are, and take steps to make it happen. This will translate easily into your romantic partnership.

You have made it to the end of the book and certainly gained some insights on cultivating lasting relationships and happiness. Know that you have a cheer leader in me, rooting for your success in love. I have no doubt you already have what it takes deep down to find and keep love in your life—my role is to help you recognize and utilize it to your advantage. One of the best parts of my day is reading and hearing success stories from others. Today, I am extending that same invitation to you. Check back in with me. After you have applied all or some of the chapters in this book, check back in with me. Send me an email or reach me on my social media platforms with your milestones and feedback. I cannot wait until the day we feature your love story on *For Better*. Until then, I challenge you to strive to make your love story epic!

ACKNOWLEDGMENTS

My God. Always and forever.

My Family. Babe, thank you for your support. You listened to every half-baked idea I bounced off you—this book, Love'n You or ForBetter, and you always responded with genuine encouragement. I also appreciate every time you would take the kids for walks just so I could concentrate. My babies, thank you for letting Daddy distract you while I worked. You all have an incredible hold on my heart.

My Mentors. Mama Rose, I value your friendship and I definitely drew from your quiet strength to stay focused and balance everything. Dr. Cynthia James, I cherish each minute you take to counsel and share life with me. I am so honored to have met you. Aunty Bose, you have covered me for nearly two decades, and if God tarries, I will continue to repay your kindness from a place of deep gratitude.

My Support System. Faith, from the first day I told you I was thinking about writing a book, you checked on my progress regularly to ensure I had not slacked off (which I had). You rock! Hadassah, the many times you graciously occupied your nephew during the first phase of this book so I could work undisturbed did not go unnoticed. Diane Gyimah. Girl! I am so grateful for your love and support throughout this entire project, including proofing posts I threw your way.

My Inspiration. The couples who lent their stories to my readers and the ForBetter audience. You are the real motivators. You, the reader. Thank you for taking this journey with me and becoming part of the Love'n You family.

BIBLIOGRAPHY

Alder, Shannon. *300 Questions to Ask Your Parents Before It's Too Late.* Springville, Utah: Horizon Publishers, 2011.

Appelbaum, Binyamin and Robert Pear, "U.S. Household Income Rises to Pre-Recession Levels, Prompting Cheers and Questions," *New York Times*, September 12, 2018, https://www.nytimes.com/2018/09/12/us/politics/median-us-household-income-increased-in-2017.html

Badhshah, Billoo. *The Unofficial Joke Book of Smart Couples.* New Delhi: Fusion Books, 2004.

Fry, Richard. "Young adult households are earning more than most older Americans did at the same age." Pew Research Center, December 11, 2018. https://www.pewresearch.org/fact-tank/2018/12/11

/young-adult-households-are-earning-more-than-most-older-americans-did-at-the-same-age/

Gladwell, Malcom. *Outliers: The Story of Success.* New York: Back Bay Books, 2011.

Grazi, Jack V. *A Laugh a Day Will Keep the Doctor Away!* Self-published, Xlibris Corporation, 2010.

Jasiekiewicz, Anne. *A Laugh a Day: Jokes to Keep the Doctor Away.* Self-published, AuthorHouse, 2010.

Jokes-Best. "Funny Family Jokes." Retrieved 2008. http://www.jokes-best.com/family-jokes.php?screen=6

Joy Online. "Just for laughs." December 12, 2014. https://www.myjoyonline.com/news/just-for-laughs/

Kintz, Jarod. *$3.33 (the title is the price).* Translated by Dora J. Arod. Self-published, Amazon.com Services LLC, 2011.

Luscombe, Belinda, "Happy People Make Their Spouses Healthier," *TIME: TIME Guide to Happiness 2020,* https://time.com/collection/guide-to-happiness/4506490/happy-people-make-their-spouses-healthier/

McGinn, Dave. "Couples who wait report better sex lives." *The Globe and Mail*, December 22, 2010. http://www.theglobeandmail.com/life/the-hot-button/couples-who-wait-report-better-sex-lives/article1847555/

Minkoff, David, comp. *Jewish Jokes: A Clever Kosher Compilation.* New York: Macmillan, 2011.

Morgan, Christine. *Know My Worth Journal.* Self-published, CreateSpace Independent Publishing Platform, 2014.

NKJV Hugs Bible for Women. Thomas Nelson Inc, 2008.

Verano, Frank. *All Kinds of Humor: Jokes, Quips, and Fun Stuff for Many Occasions over Forty Categories Book II.* Self-published, Xlibris Corporation, 2012.

ABOUT THE AUTHOR

Lily B. Donkor is passionate about building resources and providing services that facilitate thriving relationships. She has been married for eleven years to Rev. David Donkor, and takes pride in living an authentic love life they (and God) would be pleased with at the end of their lives. They currently live in Canada with their three (3) children: David II, DiorRose and Declan. Lily enjoys eating out and doing puzzles. This is her first book.

www.ingramcontent.com/pod-product-compliance
Lightning Source LLC
Chambersburg PA
CBHW031122080526
44587CB00011B/1072